girlosophy

REAL GIRLS' STORIES

anthea paul

ALLEN&UNWIN

CONTENTS

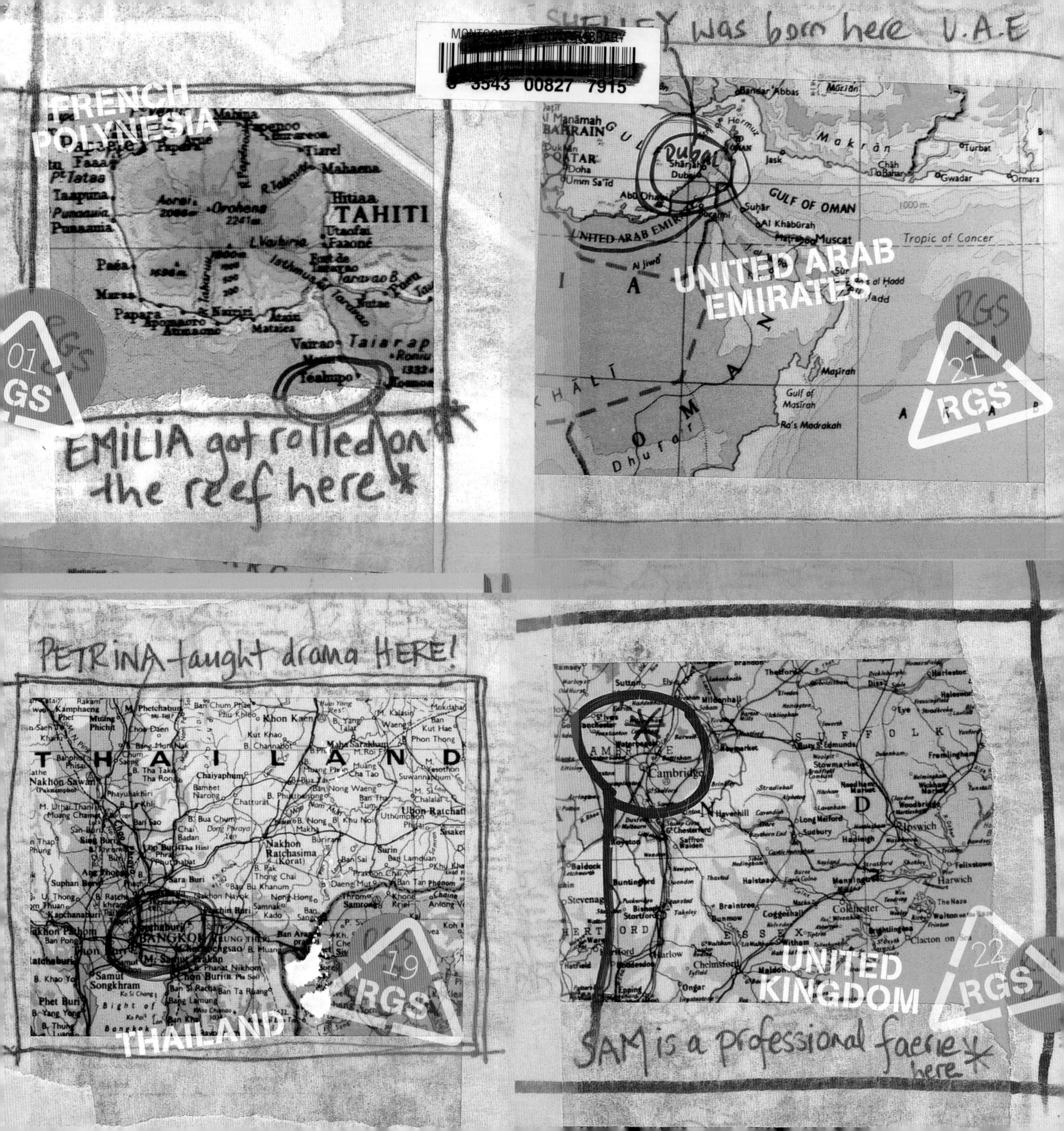

SHELLEY was born here U.A.E
FRENCH POLYNESIA
TAHITI
01
RGS
EMILIA got rolled on the reef here *
UNITED ARAB EMIRATES
GULF OF OMAN
Tropic of Cancer
Dubai
21
RGS
PETRINA taught drama HERE!
THAILAND
BANGKOK
19
RGS
UNITED KINGDOM
Cambridge
22
RGS
SAM is a professional faerie here *

First published in 2004

Allen & Unwin
83 Alexander Street
Crows Nest NSW 2065
Australia
Phone: (61 2) 8425 0100
Fax: (61 2) 9906 2218
Email: info@allenandunwin.com
Web: www.allenandunwin.com

A catalogue record for this book is available from the National Library
ISBN 1 86508 906 0

Concept by Anthea Paul
Art Direction and Design by Justine O'Donnell for jmedia design, Sydney, Australia
Additional Art Direction by Anthea Paul
Photography by Anthea Paul
Additional photography by Sean Davey (pp 10-11), Kin Kimoto (p 14), Andre B. Murray (pp 42-49), Dave Stewart (pp 84, 85), Loz Smith (p 120), Steve Doick (p 121), and Ashley de Prazer (pp 145-153)
Printed by Everbest Printing Co. Ltd, China

10 9 8 7 6 5 4 3 2 1

INTRODUCTION

Welcome to REAL GIRLS' STORIES, the girlosophy reportage book that specifically focuses on and portrays girls and young women from around the world. Based on interviews and quotes from real girls, REAL GIRLS' STORIES shines the spotlight on the experiences, thoughts, beliefs, hopes and concerns of girls in our midst as they face the reality of life as young women in the 21st century.

With the rise of the cult of celebrity over the past few decades, all of us are increasingly (over)exposed to images and stories of people who, for the most part, act or live in ways that are too far removed from our own life experience. This has left a gaping hole for those who could rightly be considered role models or true leaders for us to aspire and look up to. There are many worthy individuals who would be far more appropriate for hero worship out there, but they are not reported on nearly enough.

Many young women today are looking towards popular media icons as being some sort of benchmark. However, with such mass-marketed figures, as their new idols are, many are also ending up dealing with a variety of issues from overspending to eating disorders, not to mention various levels of addiction and self-destructive behaviors, in their attempts to emulate those who dominate the cultural landscape.

As I have said before in earlier girlosophy books and calendars, it is my firm belief that the best role models are those whom we can relate to and understand. Each person we meet possesses qualities or an approach to life that we can learn from. And on closer inspection, the most humble and the most accomplished have much in common.

Through my travels to many parts of the world, including war zones and underdeveloped regions, I have met and been inspired by many young women. Often they have had little to no contact with the world outside their own, and are thus inured, ironically, to its demands. Some are quiet achievers who have never received any sort of recognition for what they do, nor do they seek it. Some are focused on a personal goal, which matters only to them. While others are content with what they have, however it looks to outsiders. They are REAL GIRLS. It is usually the people we know - other girls, friends and family members - who are the ones that get us through when things get rugged. It is they who guide us when we need a steady hand and who contribute to our enduring sense of who we really are.

Learning from the experiences of others - for better or worse - helps us to become more confident and competent in handling whatever is thrown our way on our individual journeys. REAL GIRLS' STORIES is designed to give you a glimpse into other girls' lives. Once armed with new wisdom, it is my profound hope that each of us may better reflect upon and perceive our own lives with a gentle compassion and tolerance.

Personal and intimate, yet full of a practical resolve and a general positiveness, our featured girls offer their perspective on many subjects. They speak of family matters, love and the role of the heart, work and studies, the future, a sense of their unique purpose and destiny, and of their understanding of the mystical side of spirituality.

Readers should note that the girls featured in REAL GIRLS' STORIES were not in any way 'singled out', nor did I deliberately set out to find certain 'types' of girls. There is no casting process for girlosophy girls, rather all the girls somehow naturally connected with me or came into my world. In some cases they simply wrote and asked to be involved!

Whether it happened through a crossing of paths in a far-flung country or via a mutual friend or contact closer to home, it was destiny.

The questions posed were never formulaic, we simply had conversations and each interaction was unique. The result was a learning of the beauty of every person I have worked with on this project. The personal revelations and the access they gave me have made this book and given it an authenticity, not to mention a beating heart, and a joyful, vibrant spirit. Even more profound is my gratitude for what I have learned from each of them. To me, it is reflective of the fact that if you take the time and dig a little deeper with everyone you encounter, you will discover much to be fascinated with and inspired by. I could not have asked for better teachers.

REAL GIRLS' STORIES celebrates and salutes the role model in all of us. Our common experience as humans unites us, and to progress we must acknowledge all aspects of it, from the sweetest and smallest to the strangest and hardest. For, famous or not, prosperous or not, isolated or not, we each have much to teach. And much to learn.

I would personally like to thank each of the wonderful people who so generously gave me their time, trust and, of course, their personal stories for this project. It is a privilege and an honor to know each of you.

Anthea Paul
May 2004

Mojave Desert, California
September 2003

REAL GIRLS MAKE THE BEST ROLE MODELS FOR REAL GIRLS

DEDICATION

This book is dedicated to the memory of Misty Ellis, a real girl who is no longer here on earth with us, but whose essence and spirit always will be.

NAME: MISTY ELLIS
NATIONALITY: AUSTRALIAN
LIVED: YALLINGUP
OCCUPATION: MOTHER / DAUGHTER / SURFER

Her love for her son Jai and for her family, was closely followed by her love for the surf.

Misty started surfing at a very young age, competing by the time she was 12. She was an inspiration and role model to all female surfers.

May her spirit live on, surfing the waves forever.

Father – Ron Ellis

WE had a ceremony for Misty overlooking a place called Vic Point Bay in South Africa, about a month and a half after she died. It's probably one of the best surf spots in South Africa, and on this particular day it was just pumping surf. A whole bunch of friends from Dunsborough met up. There were about five of us. We'd all been surfing and we walked to the top of a mountain at sunset. None of us had been to her funeral. We went up there to say goodbye to Misty, even though at the time we didn't know how we were going to do it. We all decided to have a chat one on one to Misty, about what she meant to us. People cried and we hugged each other. And then we yelled out: "We love you Misty!" By the end of it, there was this incredible thick mist and fog. It had a backlit fire color and it was coming towards us. It was like Misty herself was coming towards us. She was there with us – hearing us – and we all couldn't believe it. Misty affected a lot of people. No one really understood how she affected so many people until after she died. She was very real, she had her point of view and she just stuck to that. Misty was always herself and she had no agendas. She loved her little boy Jai so much. She really had what it took to be an amazing surfer and she loved where she lived. She was on her way home when they had the car accident.
She was coming home. And now she always will be.

Friend – Romy Campbell-Hicks

IN MEMORY OF
MISTY ELLIS

NAME: EMILIA PERRY
D.O.B: 24.05.80
AGE: 24 YEARS OLD
NATIONALITY: PORTUGUESE / AUSTRALIAN
LIVES: THE NORTH SHORE, OAHU, HAWAII
OCCUPATION: BODYBOARDER / SURFER / WAITRESS

01
RGS

The first time I met Emilia was around a huge desert campfire on a beach on the Indian Ocean. With her aquiline features and thick long hair I completely expected her to have an exotic accent to match. Her broad Aussie accent – a classic – therefore came as a total surprise. Emilia laughs all the time, and along with her Hawaiian-born husband, Tamayo, manages to find the hilarious side to any situation. Their answering phone always has something crazy on it when you want to leave a message! She is what you would call a trouper – she always gives anything she attempts her very best shot. She is also the kind of genuinely nice and humble person who will help anyone who asks. A talented bodyboarder and surfer, who – when she's not pulling in to radical barrels in Hawaii or Tahiti or having her bare skin dragged across the most dangerous reefs in the world – is busy working out how she can get time off for when the next swell is forecast. No stranger to hard work, Emilia has overcome personal adversity and numerous physical setbacks in her life. But she always bounces back.

She's that kind of girl.

TOUGH CUTE
ATHLETIC
SWEET GRITTY
FUNNY QUIRKY
DETERMINED
HAPHAZARD
HONEST
LOVELY
WATER-LOGGED

My maiden name is Da Silva. My mother is Portuguese and my father is from Brazil. I speak Portuguese and love everything about the country – I love the food and I have traveled to Portugal five times.

They never married each other, but my Mum married after she and my father split up. My sister was seven and I was about six when they separated. My Mum was a single mum for a while. I remember she worked about five jobs at once.

I grew up in the suburbs of Perth. I have an older sister and a younger step-brother from my mother's marriage. For two years I went to an all-girls' school. I had to commute for three hours a day – it was two buses and two trains every school day for two years! Then I changed to a Catholic school that was five minutes from home. That was when my world changed and I began bodyboarding after school because I had more time. I was about thirteen. No one in my family surfed at all, so they couldn't understand why, when I had a choice between being in the state soccer team and bodyboarding, I chose bodyboarding. For me, it was an easy choice – the locations were much better for surfing! [laughs] Mum would sometimes say to me, "What are you doing? You'll never get anywhwere through surfing!"

Dad was more ambitious and he was harder on me. He wanted me to go to college. But he just wanted the best for me, even though he doesn't really understand about my lifestyle and my surfing either. We are not as much in communication since I got married. He has re-married as well and now I have another half-brother. My relationship with my Dad is pretty strange – more friendly than deep.

Mum understands my lifestyle better these days, but I have never felt life was about being ambitious. To me it has always been about your personal world, your inner soul and how happy you are… not how much stuff you've got!

The defining thing for me at school was a feeling of wanting to leave and counting down the days! [laughs] During Schoolies Week [the week when everyone has parties to celebrate leaving school], **I wasn't partying, I was planning! I was looking for a job so I could move to Margaret River, three hours south of Perth.**

I was always fascinated by traveling. I had the travel bug at twelve years old, after my first trip to Portugal. I believe that world is my oyster! Traveling allowed me to see my family and check out the history of Portugal, all the beautiful castles and other scenery. **MOVING OUT OF HOME AND LIVING IN ANOTHER AREA FOR ME WAS JUST AS EXCITING. IT WAS ALL NEW AND I WANTED TO DO IT AS SOON AS I COULD.** If I want something, I'll put my head down and see what I can do. I tend to just go for it – I can be very motivated if the prize is worth it!

When I arrived in Margaret River I lived in a caravan in the Margaret River Caravan Park for about eight months and I got a job pumping petrol [gas]. I worked about four days a week. It was a horrible shift, from four in the morning until four in the afternoon. **I WAS HIGH FOR ABOUT FOUR DAYS A WEEK ON THE FUMES FROM THE PETROL! BUT IT WAS A GOOD JOB FOR ME, BECAUSE YOU WERE THEN OFF FOR FOUR DAYS SO I COULD GO SURFING OR DO WHATEVER.**

Then I moved to a place near Margaret River called Northpoint, where I lived for three years. I could see the surf from my house, which I shared with a bunch of people. Of the four rooms in the house, the room I was given when I first arrived had no windows. I called it "The Dungeon" and I had to wait for three months for an upgrade! It was comedy – I would ask my flatmates every day, "Are you leaving?" It was a fun if slightly crazy household though. One of my housemates picked wildflowers for a living and he had to walk through the heaviest Australian landscape to get them. He was struck by lightning – twice! He would bring all these spiders back into the house with all the wildflowers, so I had to learn to live with spiders. Sometimes it got a bit freaky, but he would never let us kill them because he believed it was bad luck.

My first trip to Hawaii was in the winter of 1998-99. I met Tamayo on my first trip. He is Mexican / Russian / Scottish / Filipino and he was named after a famous warrior from The Philippines. **We really liked each other from the start** but I was sure we weren't going to see each other again – or

at least for a long time. Long distance relationships are too hard. But I went into one anyway. So we started traveling back and forth between Margaret River, Indonesia and Hawaii. It was the best of all worlds for both of us, because we were traveling together, living together and surfing together everywhere. It was hard to be away from him.

One night when we were on the north shore [of Oahu, Hawaii], he took me to the beach at Pipeline and he did the one-knee thing in the sand! About a week later, on New Year's Eve in 2001, we got married. We both believe if you're going to do it, you may as well do it straightaway. We just had a priest, Tamayo's mother and a witness. **MARRIAGE IS MORE SYMBOLIC REALLY.** I always feared I might jinx myself if I had a huge elaborate wedding!

And so now we are stuck together 24-7 [laughs]. We're stoked on each other! It can be a bit rugged at times – **we don't stay in luxury, most of the time a tent is home!** We don't care about that though and you just learn to be organized. As long as we're getting barreled![laughs] We do everything together and we love our lifestyle.

Tamayo has really helped me to learn the ocean too. We go to Tahiti every year for the season, to a place called Teahupoo, where they have the biggest and heaviest waves on the planet. I used to have fear, but now I know that you have to want to take-off more than you are scared not to! And you have to know your abilities, skills and your limits and act within those boundaries. But above all, you have to have the willingness to drop in. **YOU NEED A HUGE DESIRE TO GO OVER THE EDGE!**

The one thing that really changed my life forever and brought us much closer was when I was traveling in Mexico. I was with two friends – Tamayo wasn't with me at the time – and we were driving back in a rent-a-car from Todos Santos to Cabo San Lucas. We went down a hill and came across cattle crossing the road, but the brakes failed. We couldn't swerve – there was nowhere to go – and we hit this massive cow, which died on impact. I was in the front passenger seat and I hit the dashboard of the car. My girlfriend in the backseat managed to hold onto the handle in the back seat, and the driver hit the steering wheel. I was badly injured. My face split completely – I had no nose. Luckily, an American guy was driving along the same road shortly afterwards and he helped me to get to a nearby local hospital.

It was pretty much a "Happy Hack stitch job" there and even though I was in shock, I knew I had to get to California. I had medical insurance but they wouldn't discharge me until I had paid the bill, which was thousands of U.S. dollars! I couldn't even talk and so the driver of the car somehow managed to pay them. They had given me drugs for pain relief but I was totally in shock. **My focus was just that I was glad to be alive and that I knew I had to get out of there somehow.** With my friends helping me, I managed to get onto a plane! I flew to a hospital in California. About four days later, a plastic surgeon there gave me ten metal plates in my nose.

I'VE BEEN ROLLED ON THE REEF AT TEAHUPOO IN TAHITI.

I got seven stitches in my head for that. My knee has gone out, I've cut my feet many times, ripped my back open on coral (also on the Teahupoo reef), taken chunks off my knees at Pipeline in Hawaii. Disclocated my knee at Pipe too … and then there was my big accident…

I'M GOING TO BE WAY MORE STOKED KNOWING THAT I LIVED BY SOMETHING, AND THAT I DID THE RIGHT THING AS A HUMAN BEING.

Tamayo flew out from Hawaii to come and look after me, and some of my friends came to support me. I needed it by then – my head was completely swollen and I looked so bad. Tamayo didn't care about how I looked, he was just so relieved that I was alive. The accident brought me closer to everything – to God, Tamayo, my friends, and it made me appreciate my life so much more. **As a result of the accident, I make the most of every day. I love the daily challenge! And now I enjoy relaxing more too, I think it's a really important thing to do.**

We live in a small cottage at what is known as "Backyards" on the North Shore. It is called that because of its proximity to the surf break it is named after. I love living in Hawaii, but it's not always the picture postcard cliché! It's a rural area out here and you get power outages all the time. Also we have a bit of a crime problem, especially with "Ice" or crystal methamphetamine, which is so addictive that there are now a lot of "iceheads" in Hawaii. And that brings all the crime. A girl of about my age – another surfer – was abducted near where I live. Now, all the girls in our area have just introduced a buddy system for safety. Hawaii is not fun and safe, you have to be careful.

PEOPLE RUN AWAY FROM THEIR PROBLEMS and think it will all be better when they get to Hawaii. They have this myth in their heads that they will find Paradise or something and everything will be better for them here. But really, the truth is, when people run away from their problems they bring those problems with them.

I'm a Christian and I believe in God. Prayer is awesome, it protects me. I believe that God is there with me when I'm surfing big gnarly waves! I feel protected by my faith. **TAMAYO GOT ME ON FIRE FOR THE GOOD LORD!**

I love going to Church every Sunday. My soul feels really good afterwards. It is my ritual. I have to give back – God has looked after me every time I am in need. There will always be times you feel let down, but it's not necessarily when you want the help that you get it. God gives you what's best for you at the time.

The morals and the concepts of the Christian faith have been a guiding force in my life. And whether the whole thing is true or not [formal religion] I'm going to be way more stoked knowing that I lived by something, and that I did the right thing as a human being. **To me it feels so much more rewarding and positive to know that we're going somewhere better when we die.**

HER STORY:

I spotted Yuki the classic way - while she was working as a waitress in a Sushi Train! Apart from being impossibly sweet and alluring, Yuki is an anomaly, considering the strict traditional upbringing she has had. She has traveled widely, experiencing different countries and cultures, including Thailand, India, Indonesia, England, Korea, Australia and the United States. She has developed a keen interest in watersports but has had to learn about the ocean. The achievement she is most proud of is learning English!

I was born in Yokohama City in Japan. My family still lives there and I went to school there. I am the youngest child and I have one older brother, who is four years older than me. After I left school I studied English Literature at Kanto Gakuin University. I am a graduate! **My studies gave me my enthusiasm for the English and Western cultures.**

My parents are traditional in many ways and they are also Protestant. They go to church every Sunday. But they are different in their way too because most Japanese follow the Bukyo religion [a buddhist religion in Japan]. I have not decided yet about which one I prefer. It's not a popular thing for the younger generation to go to church. It's boring if you really don't feel like going! My parents are happy for me to choose whatever I would like, but I think they would be happy for me to choose to be Protestant. **My belief in religion is complicated - I'm not that interested really.** I think humans originally were from the apes, like Darwin theorized. I learned about it at school!

竹本有希
たけもとゆーき

02
RGS

NAME: YUK[illegible]AKEMOTO
D.O.B: 20.06.77
AGE: 28 YEARS OLD
NATIONALITY: JAPANESE
LIVES: YOKOHAMA, JAPAN
OCCUPATION: WAITRESS /
RECEPTIONIST

I believe that we live our life as best we can and the reality is how we find it and how we create it.

I am almost athéist, but it is a difficult question for me to say finally what I am.

I went on an extended holiday to Australia, it has been for over one year and by the time I go home to Japan, it will be closer to eighteen months. The major thing on this trip has been for me to learn to speak English. On other trips I only spoke Japanese and that was hard in some countries. I'm still learning though, I can't always understand what is being said to me yet.

I quit my job to go traveling. I used to work as a receptionist in a medium-sized hotel in Yokohama. I wanted to relax and be on holiday. I did not want to work so hard all the time. I especially wanted to learn English. It was important to me. The best way to do that is to travel and talk to people on the way. So between the ages of twenty and twenty-five, I went to Thailand, India, Indonesia, England, the United States, Korea and Australia. Australia is my biggest trip so far. It's been a big trip in so many ways for me, because

for the first time I am living away from home.

I always used to live with my parents, so now I have learned to be on my own and to live on my own. I have become independent. That has been a very different life experience to the life I had before when I was in Japan. My parents worry of course. When I first went traveling they called me almost every day! [laughs] But I managed to get them down to three times a week.

Traveling in a country or arriving anywhere for the first time is always scary. For me, India was the most scary of all the places I have been. I went there with a girlfriend – it was just the two of us. We went backpacking the first time. I paid too much money for a taxi from the airport and I lost a lot of money. I was really upset because I had been robbed – the driver knew I had made a mistake and he still took the money anyway. So I didn't trust anyone after that! And it was really hard for me to enjoy myself from then. Now, I think I would like to go back there and try again. It is the most interesting country I have been to. I'd like to try again before I get married – now that my English is better – hopefully …

I have to do a lot more on my own!

My boyfriend is Japanese. I met him while we were traveling. He is from the countryside, from a place called Okinawa. It is an island in the south. We live together at the moment, but when we are back in Japan it is going to be really hard for us to be together. Okinawa Island is about a two-hour flight from my home in Yokohama.

My parents hope I live with them again before marrying. I hope to live with them again too – it's a normal Japanese custom to do that.

My boyfriend wants to get married, but we've only been living together three or four months and it's all going to change when we get home to Japan. I worry what's going to happen when we get back, but I'll have to wait and see.

There are a lot of pressures on young girls in Japan – especially for the girls aged between fourteen and eighteen years old. Beauty and love are the biggest problems for them. It happens a lot in Japanese culture – that the girl likes someone and the love is unrequited. And then she can become very depressed. It's a cultural problem. Japanese girls are traditionally shy and have a hard time to show their feelings. It's changing a bit, now they show their feelings a bit more easily and so they become attractive to men. But ten years ago, it wasn't the case. These days it's more like the Western interaction between the two sexes. Also, the relationship between the generations – between parents and children – is a big problem. The parents are not as strong, they don't have as much of a hold over children as they used to.

My parents are actually very strict but I believe parents should have the control until the child gets a job. Once they are independent, children should be able to do what they want. But I realize that things are very different for me than for my mother, when she was my age. My parents have been together for thirty-one years. **I think they are happy, but I have many more opportunities than my mother had.** She got married young at around the age of twenty-two and had my brother straightaway.

Respect is the most important thing. For young people these days, it's something they have to learn when they get a job. When they go to work in a company, they're working with older people who they have to learn to respect.

We believe you should respect your elders. They have lived longer than we have!

But young people are getting more respect too. Personally I have respect for everybody I meet – as much as I can, I try to respect each person as they are and as they present to me.

But if someone doesn't treat me well, I don't say anything in case they get angry! It depends on the person, but I usually keep quiet. It's better!

03 RGS

NAME: RADHA MELIS
D.O.B: 21.02.84
AGE: 20 YEARS OLD
NATIONALITY: AUSTRALIAN
LIVES: MANLY, NSW, AUSTRALIA
OCCUPATION: HARE KRISHNA DEVOTEE / ASPIRING PHOTOGRAPHER

Hare Kri
Krishna Krish
Hare Rama

HER STORY:

I met Radha one muggy day in Coolangatta, on Queensland's famous Gold Coast on the north-east coast of Australia. I was there to photograph a surfing contest. On this particular day the event had been postponed due to a cyclone weather system that had been beating the coastline for a few days. Parking my rental car in front of a bank on the main street, I immediately spotted Radha, who was formally and impeccably dressed and standing out the front of the bank. This would not seem noteworthy except for the fact that Coolangatta is a fairly conservative small town - it's not exactly Byron Bay - and pretty much the most radical thing anyone sees here is the odd punk surfer or overly tattooed backpacker. But here was this vision in a turquoise sari and robe with face chalk and a matching [illegible] on her forehead, handing out leaflets to passersby about the Hare Krishna tradition. And while in one sense she was completely incongruous in that bland retail setting, she blended in perfectly with the cyan corporate signage behind her. It was as if she had picked out the colors of her attire and her backdrop deliberately, so perfect was the match. On reflection later I decided it was an unconscious and more intuitive choice than that: the color turquoise represents the fifth chakra energy and is associated with the throat. In the Sanskrit tradition the throat is the centre of spiritual communication. And this is exactly what Radha was doing - communicating spiritually to people in the street - in her [illegible] and low-key way. She looked [illegible] turns heads and is completely unaware of the effect. After spending time with her I worked out that it's an energy thing - **she simply radiates an irresistably pure form of energy. It's who she is.**

Rama Rama Hare Hare
Hare Rama Hare

My sister and I were both born into and brought up in the Hare Krishna movement. My mother joined the Hare Krishnas at the age of eighteen and she is still in it. She goes to the programs, she reads the philosophy and she chants because chanting is a big part of our religion. We have the same guru. Our guru is Sri Srimad Bhaktivedanta Narayan Maharaja. Mum gave us the freedom to choose for ourselves - there was no pressure. We had always accepted the religion, so as we got older we chose it anyway. You could say we "researched ourselves", then we chose it as a way of life and made a commitment to it. It felt right for both of us. My sister feels the same. It's good having her around as we read spiritual books together.

I know where I am going in life and I have a strong direction. To know and feel this, is very special. I know that there's something for me after this body, after this life. Everything we experience in this body is determining what's happening in this life and the next. To equal it - to balance it all - is like paying back your debts. That's the basis of our belief in karma. Karma is long-term not short-term.

I feel that I'm more at peace than a lot of others at my age. It's hard to say by comparison - because you never know what someone else is feeling - but I'm very happy with what I've chosen. I feel happier than what that seems to be or what it seems to mean for other people. And I have a large family! Some of my friends who aren't devotees say, "You're so lucky, you have friends all over the world and wherever you go you have family to stay with everywhere!" As a devotee we regard all other devotees as being our family and spiritually this is very special for me.

My birth family influences me and my Hare Krishna extended family does too. I think in having a big family you develop a sense perhaps of who you are. It teaches you a lot of tolerance because you understand where different people are coming from. And you soon learn that everyone is on their own path. Compassion is also something that you learn.

My family is a little complicated [laughs]… no not really! I have three younger half-sisters and one older sister. In fact, she's my half-sister too but we were raised together by my [biological] father, so to me she's just my sister. Actually they all are! My younger half-sister's name is Jahnavi, which is another name for the Jamuna River in India, and I am named after Radha, who is a Goddess, and the consort of our God, Krishna. And I live with my older sister in a share house in Manly, in Sydney. I've just moved down from the Gold Coast where I was living with my mother in Murwillumbah. My Mum is single and happy. She's been divorced twice and she's really happy on her own. It gives her more time to do her own thing. My Dad has since re-married though - that's why I have my other, younger sisters from his marriage. My grandfather is Dutch. I was recently talking to him about his experiences in the Second World War - he went through so much! My Nanna is no longer alive. I always wish I had talked more to her. Family is a big thing for me!

I've been a vegetarian all my life. I just eat a lot of nuts, drink vegetable juices and protein shakes, and I eat fruit too. I think physically I am a lot healthier as a result of my religion. I don't drink either, so I don't go out late as I'd rather get up early and go to the beach for a swim. Being a vegetarian has been crucial for my path. I have never had a desire to eat meat. I am an animal rights activist and I believe it's not right to eat flesh.

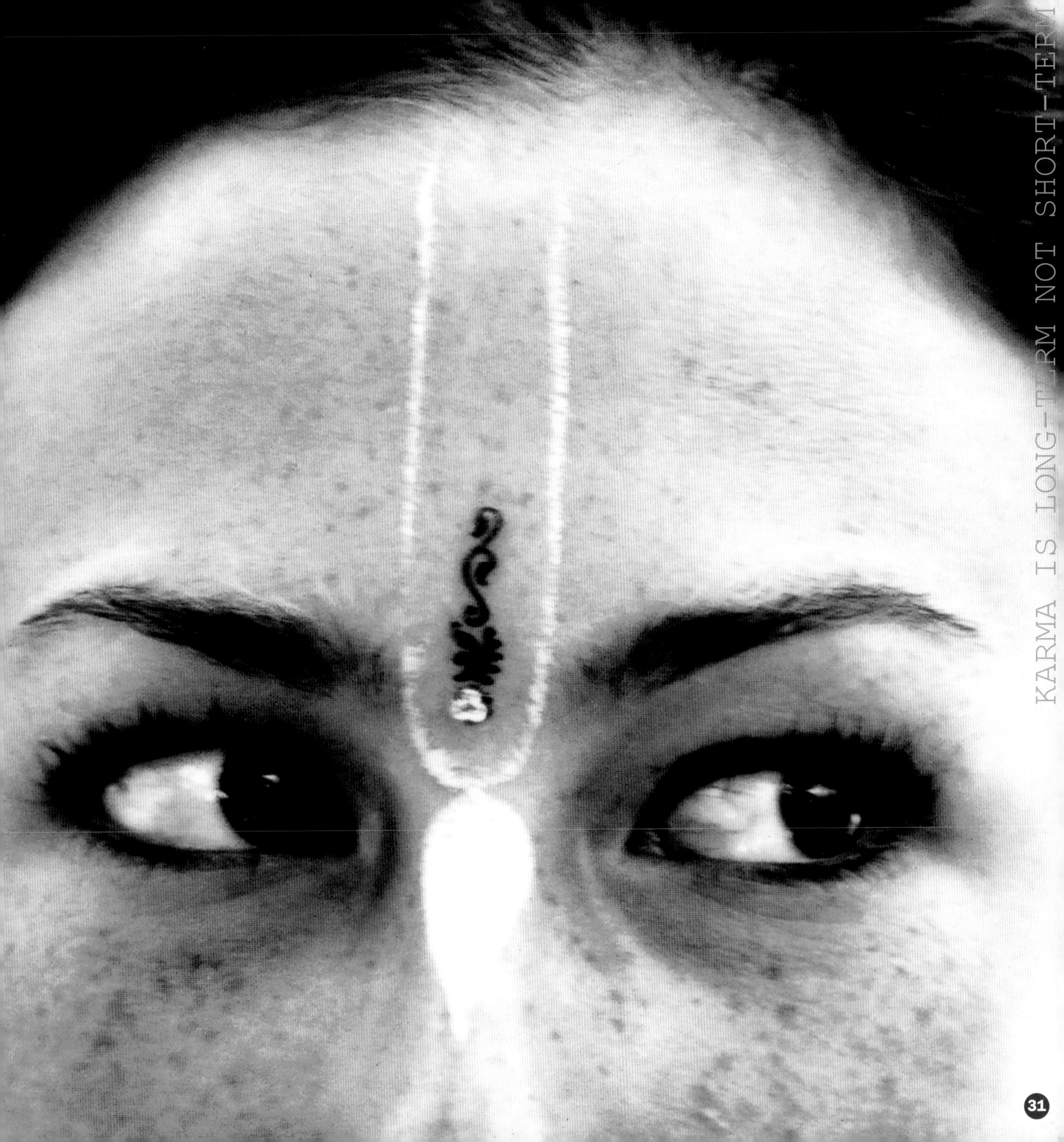
KARMA IS LONG-TERM NOT SHORT-TERM

We all have souls and so we all have the right to live. And that includes all creatures! I believe that what you do to them comes back on you - that's karma too. It's one of the main reasons for choosing vegetarianism.

I've been to India four times. I'm planning to go again later this year. My first impression was that they are crazy drivers! It's a completely different world. People are so amazingly friendly, **they appear to have nothing, but in a way they have everything**. The first time I went to a village town called Navadweep, near Calcutta. I went to a festival that was held in March, which Hare Krishna devotees from all over the world attend. We do a sort of pilgrimage - it's called "Parikram" - and we visit sacred places together as a huge group. It's a walk led by my guru. If you can imagine about five hundred Western devotees and about ten thousand Bengalis [Indian devotees who live in West Bengal] all walking around together! And there is another festival around September/October, and for this Parikram we visit all the sacred places belonging to our Gods, Krishna and Radha, who I am named after, with all the devotees. More Western devotees come to this festival. It's a slightly bigger event that runs for six to eight weeks. Once we are on the Parikram, we move around camping, staying in dharamsalas everywhere we go. I love it so much because I have so much fun with all my friends - **you're doing something spiritual with your friends - who are all into the same things too.**

In the October Parikram 2003, I had to carry the offerings. It is a ritual that everyone offers obeisances [offerings to the gods] and bathes in the river for purification. This takes place at Radha Kunda, which is a lake where the Goddess Radha broke her bangle in half. Radha Kunda is therefore "her" lake and it is considered to be more holy than the Ganges River. The whole thing was special.

It gets very tiring traveling in India, and doing the Parikram is also very austere physically! You have to sit for long periods of time and you're sleeping in a room with basic facilities. We can only take cold showers, and sometimes for sleeping it's just a mat on the floor. We walk barefoot everywhere so my feet get pretty rough and calloused and dirty! But the whole thing is so much fun, you soon get used to it and after a while it doesn't even bother you. Last year, on my most recent trip there, I got sick for the first time - I actually caught dengue fever! So that was pretty bad, but the other times I've been fine, just the occasional cough or cold.

When the men wear peach, it is because they have taken a vow of celibacy. They are focused more on spiritual achievement, not on family life. When they wear white however, they are known as "Grihastas" and as such they will marry and raise children. When women wear white it means something else though. As a devotee we are supposed to only have sex within marriage, and so a lot of women when they get older or after they have had their family and so on and they want to focus on their spiritual life, they put on white to show their commitment. It's not like I would only marry someone who was a Hare Krishna devotee! But it's certainly easier to be with someone who shares the same beliefs. I wouldn't rule out anyone though. I have had a boyfriend who was a devotee but he and I are just friends now.

In Murwillumbah there's a big Hare Krishna center. We have a temple there. When I was home I was going there every day for programs, classes, worshiping the deities. When I'm in Sydney I go to the temple in North Sydney. **Some of my non-Hare Krishna friends come with me, they think it's cool that I'm into something.** And I read spiritual books a lot too, I'm currently reading *The Bhagavad Gita* from the Sanskrit literary tradition. It's a really important and beautiful spiritual book.

The classes I take are about the "Dharma". This teaches you how you should act and how to control the mind. And we do a lot of chanting and singing too. I have a Hindi and Bengali Sanskrit songbook, which is one of my favorites.

My family used to live in Chatswood in Sydney, then we moved to Murwillumbah on the Sunshine Coast, then to the Western Australian outback on a farm near Halls Creek. And then back to Murwillumbah. Living in the outback was amazing. It was something my mother always wanted to do – go buy a farm and live in the outback! I think she just wanted to have the experience, because after six months we moved back to Murwillumbah. But I was so sad to leave. All this incredible space and the desert! I loved living out there, but after a while it was this feeling of "Well, we've done that now". My Mum sells electrical power conservation systems. My Mum's quite … [pauses] she's done a lot in her life! She's really strong. She's experienced a lot and she's come through it. I always hope I don't have to go through as much stuff as she did, but I always hope that I'm as strong.

I would like to live in India for some time of each year. It's hard to live there all year round because of the cold and the heat; however, I would like to do something career-wise that gives me the opportunity to travel there. Working as a photographer would give me the ability to base myself in India at least part of the time. I have always felt that my work would have to exist alongside my spiritual life. A lot of devotees put together books and magazines, transcribe lectures etc. as a means to stay completely focused on their spiritual life. So, ideally I would love to work within the group for that reason too. And eventually I want children, but I'm in no rush to start a family.

I don't think I've had an emotional crisis really. Although I do remember being pretty devastated leaving my friends in Sydney, when I first moved away to the country, far north to Murwillumbah, which is so far from Sydney. I met them at the school I went to. I went to a Steiner School and because of the progressive program – it's balanced between arts and sciences – it was perhaps the happiest time of my childhood.

Right now is a pretty good time in my life! I've just moved back to Sydney, I'm going overseas at the end of the year, I've got lots of friends and I'm living with my sister again. I sort of feel like I'm starting a new period of my life – everything's exciting, it's a renewal period. Spiritually I feel more alive than I have for a while and I feel like there's a lot happening for me in my spiritual life. I'm more inspired and that makes me happier. In Coolangatta, when I was doing Hare Nam recently – we walk around singing on the streets. It's really fun once you forget about everyone else and I was just feeling so good about life and about myself. And my guru is coming out to Australia soon. It's always a renewal every time I see him.

I don't often get to see my guru, Sri Srimad Bhaktivedanta Narayan Maharaja, one-on-one. We mostly see him in a group and he tells wonderful pastimes [stories]. I have gone to darshan [devotees make prayers and pay homage to the guru at a certain specified time] though. He always asks you how you're going in your spiritual life. If you have needs materially or spiritually, he helps you out and he gives advice. His advice is usually to chant more, but he always wants to talk to you about any problems, and to help you sort them out. He's just turned eighty-three and he's always happy!

NAME: ANJA UHLMANN
D.O.B: 09.03.89
AGE: 15 YEARS OLD
NATIONALITY: SWISS
LIVES: BIEL, SWITZERLAND
OCCUPATION: STUDENT / BRAZILIAN DANCER

HER STORY:

Anja is a laidback girl with a distinctly philosophical outlook on life. Living in Europe, but having experienced living and studying in other countries, she speaks three languages fluently - German, French and English - and is currently learning her fourth tongue, Italian. Naturally inquisitive and by her own admission over-analytical, Anja has a cerebral take on things that is so amazing that, even if you don't believe in past lives, she could convince you. Anja is a maverick thinker who loves Brazilian dancing and enjoys reading heavyweight Buddhist textbooks. When talking to her it becomes evident that she is indeed an old soul.

AT THE
CORE OF
EVERYTHING
THERE IS NO
KNOWLEDGE.
THERE IS
JUST LOVE.

I believe there is knowledge that you can't necessarily have **in this life.**

I have lived in Switzerland all my life. I was born in Olten near Langenthal, but now I live with my mother in Biel, in the west of Switzerland. I have three half-brothers from my father's side, but I am the only child of my parents. My father and my mother were together for fourteen years.

In 2003, I went through a lot of things and many changes. It made me look at the world differently. I was asking lots of questions: Is everything how it seems? I was asking myself about life. I was starting to read a lot of books around this time. Sometimes you read it and you don't understand it and later it comes to you! It was about this time that I decided to study in the direction of psychology and philosophy.

I am in the first year of college – we call it "Gymnasium". I have finished high school and I would like to study in Geneva, in the future. It's only six months since I have been at this new school and it's very different from my former school. For a start there are one thousand people – so many new people for me to get to know. The level of discussion is much higher here as this school is for the best students. It's been a nice change – and more interesting for me to not necessarily be the one who is explaining things to others all the time. It's different being the one who listens and I can now learn something from them instead. It challenges me now! I speak three languages and I am learning a fourth, Italian. Most people in Europe speak English, German and French. That's normal for us!

We are not very religious – my Mum is Christian and she reads stuff, but it's more about praying for her. We don't believe in being punished because of sins, but we do believe in reincarnation. I have a lot to do with Buddhist monks and I have been taught that I will be here again in another life. **Some souls are differently developed because of their past lives.**

My grandmother and uncles became Buddhists and they knew these Tibetan monks from Nepal. When the monks came to visit Switzeralnd I met them. It was such a lovely experience! You can really feel their holiness and the love that comes from them. I read a lot of books on spirituality and Buddhism and you can just feel that they have no bad thoughts, there is no hatred or anger coming from them. You just feel good around them!

My favorite book on spirituality is by His Holiness, Dalai Lama. It's called *Ethics, Mindfulness and Compassion*. It's an inspiring, essential book for all people. I have gained a lot through this book as I didn't have a normal happy family life. I had to deal with the change that occurred with the breakup of my parents. It made us all sad. Many people have similar situations but I never really compare. I try not to!

And meditation helps. If I am feeling low, I meditate every day. It just helps. I did a course to learn and understand it. A friend of mine is a psychologist and she shows me ways to meditate and to do positive thinking and that really helps. It's also helpful for stress relief too. You have to find the silence!

Whenever there's a problem, meditate on it and see the solutions to the problem. Solutions come when you meditate.

For fun I practice a form of Brazilian dancing. It's known as Capoeira. It's from the days of slavery when the slaves told their keepers that they wanted to dance, but really they were practicing fighting! These days you just do it to music as a mixture between fighting and dancing. It's such a great release!

I think, particularly now with the amount of war that is going on and terrorism and so forth, the Buddhist message is very important. If I had a chance to talk to all of them [the participants in the war in Iraq and the war on terror] I would say a lot! I really don't think it's okay what anyone is doing. It's a shame they went to war. I don't understand how the terrorists can treat people without respect. Everybody is so scared now, but it's not good. **Everyone has to die eventually anyway but they are talking about it way too much. It is for their own agenda. It is barely reported if twenty thousand people die in India or in a natural disaster...** Most young people are against the war. Some are not interested though – they just want to live their lives. Some have too many problems with themselves to be interested in anyone else's life.

We have a lot of freedom in Switzerland but because of our geographical and historical position in Europe we also have a huge drug problem. I used to be together with my friends a lot, hanging out with them all the time. Drug issues came up and we had to deal with that in our group. I don't hang out as much with them these days.

We also have a big problem with suicide and depression. People get depression because of what they have experienced in their life here in Europe. There are too many homeless people living at the train station. We treat our problems differently in Switzerland, but we should still be a country with a proper social system.

In winter I am always sad, but in summer the sea and the sun just gives me energy!

THOUGHTFUL ANALYTICAL
NON-JUDGEMENTAL SHY CALM
UNPREDICTABLE A COLLECTOR
VISUAL WARY CONTENT

Los Angeles
LAMP
Los Angeles
SOUTH

05

RGS

NAME: MICHELLE HOPE SLAYBAUGH
D.O.B: 14.10.82
AGE: 22 YEARS OLD
NATIONALITY: U.S. CITIZEN
LIVES: LOS ANGELES
OCCUPATION: VOLUNTEER / PERSONAL ASSISTANT

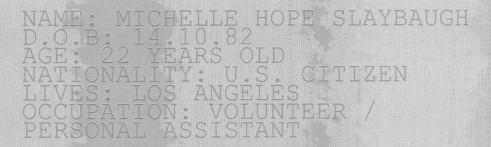

HER STORY:

I spotted Michelle at the MAGIC Hip Hop Fashion Convention in Las Vegas, Nevada, in August 2003. Wearing a camouflage beanie and pigtails in her hair and bouncing around the celebrity basketball match in progress at the time, she was a standout, even from a distance. With one eye on the action in the middle of the court – including the Playboy Playmate of the Year, and a former Miss USA in gold stilettos! – Michelle went about her job of handing out promotional merchandise in her confident, unself-conscious way, cajoling, selling and chatting to the courtside spectators. Her sheer energy made her impossible not to notice, but when she bounced up to our group and gave us beanies, it was immediately obvious that Michelle could be a beauty queen herself.

Living in, as she calls it, "the rat race that is L.A.", Michelle is one of those people who fairly burst at the seams with her stories, plans, outrageous jokes and life experience. Her middle name, Hope, sums up Michelle's attitude and what she also brings to the homeless children of a downtown Los Angeles shelter, who have come to depend upon her.

IN THE SO-CALLED CITY OF ANGELS, MICHELLE IS AN ANGEL TO MANY.

I am an only child from a single-parent family. I was born in Lafayette in Indiana. My Mom is Caucasian and Dad is African-American. When I was really young my parents separated. My Dad had some personal issues he had to deal with. At times I had anger in my heart, but I can't really blame him, we all go through our bad times, you know? I'm sure my Dad didn't mean to hurt us at the time, but it's tough every day for me to be able to accept it. I am still a bit angry about it, for my Mom though. She had to work twice as hard to look after me and to accomplish her goals. Things were very hard for her. We lived in a trailer in Indiana, West Lafayette … but it was a nice trailer. **MY MOM MADE IT COMFORTABLE AND WE HAD EVERYTHING WE NEEDED.**

When I was still in school my mother decided to go back and study at university. At the time she was working in a micro-electronics factory. They made plastic pieces for - amongst other things - bombs. During the Gulf War, my Mom worked overtime shifts at the factory because there was a lot more demand for the pieces. She worked sometimes eighteen hours a day, but she decided to quit her job and got her Masters Degree in Education. While that was happening we moved in with my grandmother. That was a happy time, Grandma was a nurse in the war - she was amazing and she has all these medals! My mom is an only child too. So it was just me, my mom and my grandmother. That was our little family!

The school I attended was mostly a white school. I always knew I was different, but when you grow up around a white culture you don't really understand how different you really are! [laughs] It wasn't until I moved to California that I gained a better understanding of my mixed heritage and that was where **I discovered diversity for the first time.**

I left high school in 2000. In April 2002 I moved out from Indiana to Los Angeles with [US]$500 in my pocket and a trunk of belongings. It was the most intense thing ever! I can remember getting in to L.A., and the first night I stayed in the downtown Holiday Inn Express. My room was on the eighth floor. And I remember staring out the windows and just seeing an endless amount of possibility in the downtown lights. I was like, "This is it! I did it, I left home!" That was the biggest moment in my life. From then on, I knew I had to take care of myself. I couldn't rely on my Mom any more. I had made the biggest leap of faith. It was THE moment. It was - man - it was Los Angeles! It was the beginning of the rest of my life.

I wanted to do merchandise marketing and I enrolled in the Fashion Institute of Design and Merchandising in downtown L.A. It was a very expensive school but my Mom helped me to get a student loan. The fees were [US]$22,000 per year. I went to school with people for whom *Harper's Bazaar* was their bible. It was all about the lifestyle, fashion, accessories, the exotic destinations - this is what you were meant to be aiming for in life! I thought it was what I wanted to do, but then I found that I couldn't relate to people in that world. The stores that these people were talking about, I could never even afford to even walk into them! The teachers and the students were all talking a different language to me, but to them it made perfect sense. I had a knack for the marketing and business side. It was easy for me! Then I started to skip class and spend more time at the homeless shelter. I dropped out of that school after ten months. **I couldn't handle these girls who would complain about not getting a [US]$2500 handbag, when I would be thinking that right down the street there were kids who don't have any food to eat.**

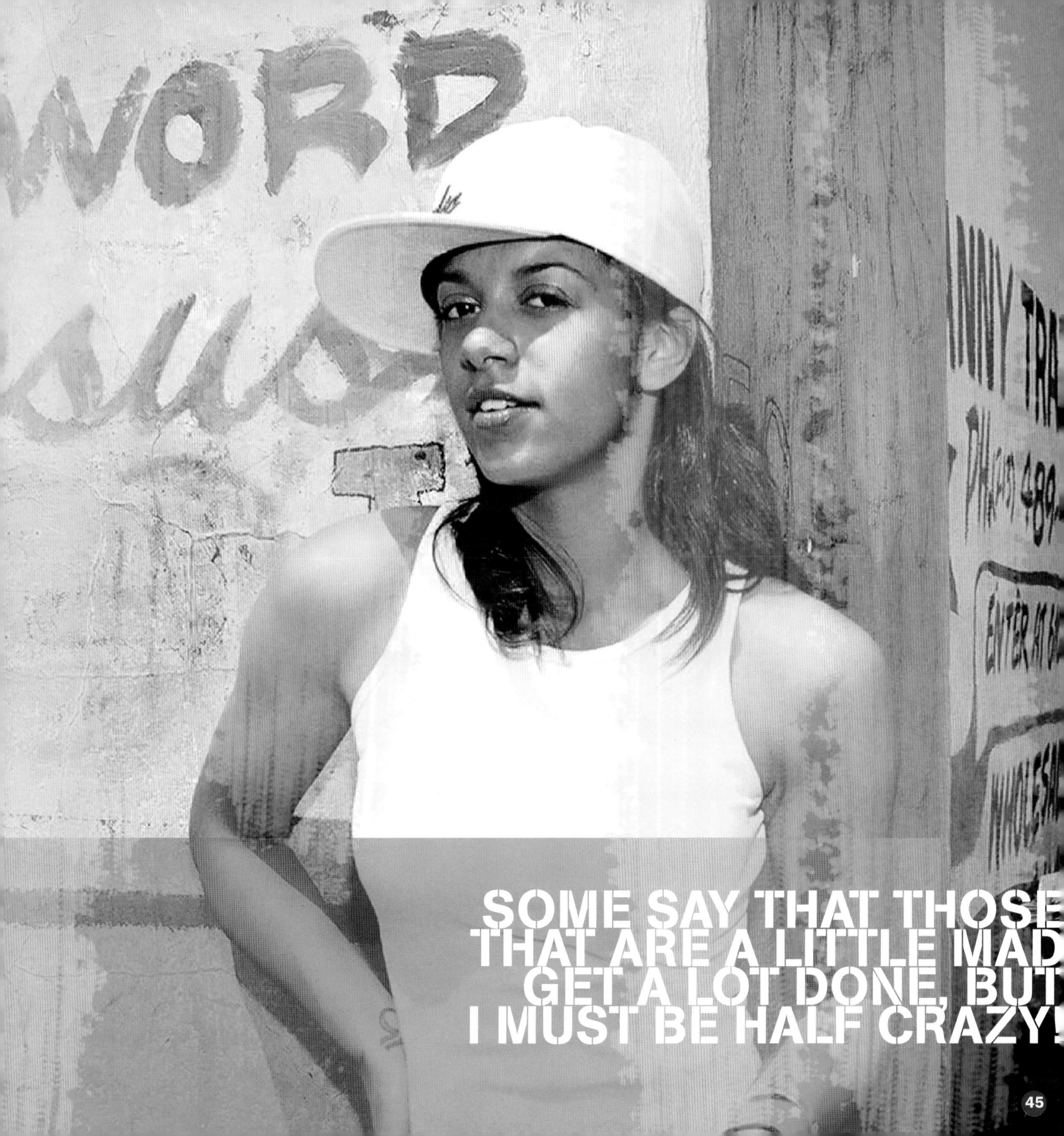

SOME SAY THAT THOSE
THAT ARE A LITTLE MAD
GET A LOT DONE, BUT
I MUST BE HALF CRAZY!

I moved out to L.A. by myself and at first it was a bit lonely. The shelter was where I felt connected and grounded. It was an outlet for me. If ever I was sad, or wasn't feeling that great, I could go always go there and re-energize.

I have done such a 360-degree turn with my life, well maybe a 320 [laughs] … I'm by no means perfect, but I definitely was really bad at certain times. In my teen years I was a rebel. I really was a bad kid! In high school I would skip school a lot, do drugs, and just party. My grades suffered. My mother and I fought a lot during this period and hated each other at times. We love each other so much now, she's an incredible person. My mother still lives in Indiana, but I only go home only once or twice a year.

The reason I turned to drugs and alcohol in high school was to try to fit in and be popular. I gave in to the peer pressure. More young people than not are succumbing to peer pressure. **IF I COULD I'D SAY TO THEM, "TAKE A DEEP BREATH AND MOVE THROUGH IT, YOU CAN MAKE IT THROUGH". I'D TELL THEM NOT TO GO THERE.** Every time they are offered ecstasy, coke, I would advise them just to say, "That's not for me!"

I can relate to any embarassing situation! [laughs] But there were also days when I would be thinking, "Oh my gosh, can it be over now?" After high school, I wasn't doing anything much with my life. I certainly did my fair share of experimenting, maybe mine and the next person's too! And when you fill in time with drugs and alcohol, you are on a fast track to nowhere.

It took me a while to do it, but until you make the conscious decision to be an adult, you won't progress. You have to accept responsibility. I grew up in a small town where some of the people I know - friends of mine - have become crackheads.

I saw kids throw their life away by doing a lot of drugs…
I have one thing to say: **"CRACK KILLS".**

I REALLY VALUE EVERYTHING I WENT THROUGH EVERY DAY. I recently went home and that was such a trip! I hadn't been home in two years. I felt like I'd stepped back in time. Everybody was doing the same old thing. Hopefully I have been progressing, maturing and growing. One night I went out with some old college friends. No way could they fathom the changes in me.

I was in a music video for a band that was on high-rotation on MTV - if you blink you might miss me - but people back home thought I was a superstar![laughs] The reality was that I had to walk sixteen blocks to get there, I only got paid [US]$75, for it and there was no food on set and no air conditioning! But back home in Indiana, people thought it was the most fabulous thing ever. I tried to give them the reality, but they just wanted the myth of L.A.

I have no illusions of glamor these days. It might be great to have a cute Mercedes Benz convertible and Jimmy Choo shoes, but what would be the point? I mean, where am I going to wear Jimmy Choos - on the train downtown to the homeless shelter, where I'm conversatin'[sic] with random homeless crackheads?

Every holiday I go to a place called the L.A. Mission, which is a Christian-based organization. We serve food to the homeless people there and we wash their feet, which is in keeping with the actions of Jesus. There is a booth called "Treat your Feet" and it is manned by volunteers, podiatrists and doctors.

It is a great program, one from which I am trying to learn as much as I can. The people at L.A. Mission are really nice. **They call Skid Row "HOPE CENTRAL".**

My dream is to open a homeless shelter by my thirtieth birthday, so I try to learn as much as I can by volunteering, learning how other organizations have set up their system. My Mom always thinks I'm amazing, she is my biggest fan.

Every time I am at a bus stop, someone changes my life. I met an eighteen-year-old Hispanic girl who inspired me so much with her life story. She nearly brought me to tears. She was in school, studying to be a dental hygienist. She went to night school while she was pregnant and the baby's father was in prison. I told her how much respect I had for her and how much she had inspired me to do better with my life. She was phenomenal. I'm trying to be as good and as motivated as she is.

I have heard stories from people on the street that blow my mind. There is so much to hear and learn from the experiences of others.

I have had so many jobs! Since the year 2000, I have been a janitor [cleaner] at a bank, a gymnastics instructor, a promotional model for this home drycleaning product in a mall.

I was a Hooter girl at Hooters [a chain of restaurants]. I've worked with the developmentally challenged, and I have worked in club promotion. I have been a topless dancer, a go-go dancer, construction worker, waitress. I've done modelling, club hostessing. I've been a door bitch … [laughs] Now that was power! I helped do a start-up company and got fired because the guy wanted to date me and I wasn't interested. I've done it all!

Stripping is not what I would ever want to do again, but I was only interested in taking care of my bills. I don't feel I have done anything to be ashamed of. Until you've walked a mile in my shoes how can you understand me? I look at it as just another part of the journey of Michelle. I started it when I had really low self-esteem. I grew up in an all-white community and no one understood me. Back home I couldn't even go to the hairdresser because they would say they didn't know how to do ethnic hair.

As I said, I would never strip again, but burlesque dancing is something I would love to do. I think being a showgirl is beautiful. **Those girls work very hard to do what they do.**

I don't believe in prostitution - but who am I to judge anyone? That's another world altogether.

I am a volunteer at a homeless shelter and I go there every Friday afternoon. I call the shelter "my little house of hope". It's in downtown Los Angeles, about four blocks from what they call Skid Row. Skid Row consists of rows of tents and people living in them full-time. It's pretty full-on — you can smell urine in the street. Originally the shelter was a hotel. There were crackheads, prostitutes and pimps staying there, and there were a lot of bad things going on. Then this woman came in and bought the hotel and turned it into a shelter. She used to charge [US]$295 per month for one room - it was really cool for people in need. It used to be under a program called Shelter First. But things are falling apart and it may become a hotel again, because the health facilities aren't up to standards for it to remain an official shelter.

Where I come from, you leave your doors unlocked! I came to the West Coast of California from West Lafayette, Indiana, two years ago. So moving from a mid-west state to a big city was a bit of a shock to say the least. I live in an area of Los Angeles, South Central, which is known to be a bad area, especially for gang activity and organized crime. **I heard an Hispanic lady on the train say that a body was recently found on 36th and 2nd Avenue, so charred and cut-up they didn't know whether it was male or female. And I hear gunshots from my house all the time. So it's a dangerous area in certain respects. But where I actually live is in an enclave - it's like a safe pocket. I live in a really lovely house and I have a roommate. And we have nice neighbors too. But one mile from me in any direction, there's probably some shady stuff going on! To remove the stigma of the suburb, the authorities have tried to re-name it South Los Angeles, but it will probably always be known as South Central.**

In downtown L.A. many people have never made it beyond grade 8 in school. They have nothing to back them up. Some of them have learning disabilities and a lot have mental illness. I've worked with these people and some you can tell there are developmental problems with them. The statistics say that seventy-five percent of homeless people have some sort of mental illness. This is poverty and isolation on another level and it's very sad.

I started working there as a volunteer mentor for a group of children. The children were very beautiful but they were so dirty! And they were very wary - there was definitely a trust issue with all of them. The parents could drop them off but someone who was responsible had to be with the children while they were at the center. It is like an after-school program and the ages went from two to sixteen — about thirty to forty children in total that I mentor. It fluctuates. My personal commitment is to go every Friday for two hours, and I go for special occasions at the shelter like easter egg decorating and stuff like that.

The kids and their parents love me! And I love them too. Even when they're naughty I still love them! I get the most gorgeous gifts — little handmade books and drawings from the kids. That's one of the joyful parts.

I entered the Miss Black California 2004 pageant and - to my complete surprise - I won it. I go to Miss Black USA in February 2005 and then I can go to other pageants if I want. I'm not much of a pageant girl really. I only wanted to win third place in the contest but I ended up winning everything! I was so amazed when I also won Best Speaker, Best Interview, Best Swimsuit, Miss Congeniality, and Miss Social Conscience. I was trying to pay off my school debt - ten months of fashion school and I still have a crazy debt – and although it didn't pay off all the debt, at least it paid off my book fees!

Presently, I am a personal assistant to a CEO of a corporation — learning management stuff — and I want to stick with it as it could be a long-term career stepping stone. It's great for networking, has good earning potential as for the future in general and in all aspects of life.

I'm at the crossroads where I've accepted adulthood. I'm working nine to five in a business suit and I attend meetings. Every experience in life is a test. The last two years have tested me. They were to find out if I was ready and mature enough to conquer the business world, or to at least get a good jump on it at an early stage. I believe with God on my side, persistence and elbow grease I will be able to open that homeless shelter.

I'm single at the moment and I doubt that will change for a while. I'm focused on other things, other goals. Everything else that I want will come along in good time.

I DIDN'T GROW UP RICH - I GREW UP IN A TRAILER PARK. BUT VISITING DOWNTOWN L.A. WAS A HEAVY EXPERIENCE WHEN I FIRST WENT THERE. IT WAS AN UNEDUCATED LEVEL OF POVERTY THAT I HAD NEVER SEEN BEFORE.

06

RGS

NAME: ASHLEY WILLCOX
D.O.B: 15.01.86
AGE: 18 YEARS OLD
NATIONALITY: AUSTRALIAN
LIVES: NARABEEN AUSTRALIA
OCCUPATION: STUDENT / ASPIRING JOURNALIST

HER STORY:

I met Ashley on the last day of a long Sydney summer in my hometown of Avalon on Sydney's Northern Beaches. It was a beautiful day, one of those days when the wind has that first winter chill on it, but it's not yet cold enough to wear a sweater or a hoodie. Even if it were winter, we wouldn't have needed to rug up - Ashley has the kind of thousand-watt smile that could heat the coldest environment! In a world that drastically needs positivity, she possesses the kind of sunny disposition and attitude that goes a long way. Ashley has a sharp mind and a clear outlook on life. Even at the relatively tender age of eighteen she has the kind of wisdom that many in their late twenties have not yet developed. It's a refreshing thing to be around someone with maturity beyond her years. Age differences melt away and conversation becomes a true exchange. Ashley has a cool perspective and a great way of looking at life and … she's just great fun to talk to.

Energetic
hyperactive
weird
independent
crazy
intelligent
friendly
kind
egalitarian
not
materialistic

In my family, education has always been a focus. My parents have always encouraged us and **I was dedicated at school** - it has been one of the solid parts of my life. When I was thirteen - on my thirteenth birthday - we moved to a new area. It was hard at first - I didn't know a soul! School became my anchor. After six months I settled in, but it was hard in the beginning to get to know people. Sometimes, because of the way I act, people assume I'm not very smart. I just muck around and act silly sometimes! So it was a shock for some when I won an award from the Minister of Education. I got a perfect score and a High Distinction for an essay I wrote on the Tiwi [indigenous tribe] and the concept of time. It was for the subject Society and Culture. I am having an excerpt of the essay published in a magazine … it's nice to have my work recognized.

Time is a difficult concept but I had so much fun researching it. I like alternative subjects. **I like thinking about the great, unanswered questions!** Whenever I'm at Tuross Heads, which is away from the city, the stars are really clear. I love lying on the grass talking about the mysteries of the universe and watching for shooting stars! Once I wished to get into university to do journalism and that's what happened. I'm in the first year of my course. I'm on my way!

My Tiwi research made me think a lot about the fact that most people in the Western world are so materialistic. I try not to be hung up on buying stuff. I hardly ever buy anything for myself, I practically have to be pressured into it. [laughs] I feel funny even wearing a bit of gold. But most people buy themselves things all the time and they don't even think about it! But I always think, why work hard all week and then just buy stuff? I guess a lot of the time people think to themselves, **"Oh, I've gotta have this to make me happy". But if you look back ten years later, you didn't really need it!**

We should look after the natural life around us instead of destroying it. All life forms have an equal weight in our whole system. For example, I don't really think people should wear fur. Fur is a rich person's folly. It's pointless to do something like that just to look good. And it might go in and out of fashion - what's the point? People always buy something and then later they change their mind … It's just this cycle of waste and everyone is hooked in.

Girls especially spend all their money after their week at work on things like acrylic nails, jewelry, beauty appointments, clothes and hair. They can go through hundreds and hundreds of dollars - their whole salary for a week - buying things to make them look good. The media creates this image and tells everyone that they have to live up to it.

Girls are just wearing less and less too. Now they wear backless and split dresses that you basically can't wear anything under. They have to use tape [for their breasts]! If you had worn something like that even a few years ago, people would have been shocked, but now it's so much in the media that it's become the norm.

But the consequences of such pressure happen on the quiet - many girls have eating disorders. Their life revolves around their Saturday night out and that's all. Maybe they think they'll meet the man of their dreams. Some of them are really open about their eating disorders and they'll say they just get tired a lot because they have anorexia. It's almost seen as a **normal rite of passage** - something that all girls have to do now, which is so sad. And the boys know that the girls have eating disorders.

Time can be thought of as a straight line or as a circle:
the linear, sequential march of days and years, or the rotation of the
seasons. Our cultural orientation has a profound effect on our daily lives.

A friend went to a wedding once and he said all the girls at the table had hiccups. They were all doing it! It's a sign of eating disorders. And another of my male friends once said to me, "I'd hate to be a girl … girls can't eat, and so they've got no energy. I feel sorry for them."

But it's all a part and a symptom of the number one problem for girls - which is that girls think they have to be beautiful. There's this impression among girls that you can be the most successful person in the world, but if you're ugly, no one will care. One of my closest friends is really beautiful and I have seen that it can be a very isolating thing. She gets a lot of unwanted attention and even though she is highly intelligent, her intelligence will never be judged as being as noteworthy or as important as her beauty. Other girls are horrible to her because she's got this perceived physical advantage. One of her strongest memories is scrubbing stuff off toilet doors that people had written about her.

I think it all comes back to the whole thing about materialism as a way of life. Beauty is just another thing you can buy. The pressure is on and the media is just so heavy. So it is understandable in a way that this is the result for young women especially. Even the way [certain young female celebrities] are being worshiped - you'd think they could save the world! The cultural icons for all young women in their late teens and early twenties are pretty thin on the ground! [laughs]

I believe that to whom much is given, much is expected. But if you're beautiful, thin, rich and don't have to do anything, it is somehow seen as the pinnacle of success. It seems as though no one really wants to do anything any more. But celebrity icons can only exist because people are unhappy.

People in society are becoming more selfish and lazy and they don't want to do something if it doesn't benefit them. They are not as caring, and being compassionate is somehow considered to be almost uncool. Young girls think that being unkind makes them hip or cool. Maybe it's just because everyone is insecure these days. What's wrong with being a kind, friendly person?

Imagine living on a little island and you don't have to compete with anyone to look good. You just have to be yourself. You don't need fashion because it would be irrelevant. I have been to a small Fijian island called Namotu a few times now. I love it so much and I always feel so confident there. My older brother lived there for a year as a fisherman and a boatman and I saw how peaceful he was after that period. Now he's working in a retail shop and it was a culture shock for him to see the money people spend! My brother is the best guy I know. We have been through a lot together and we are really close. I look up to him so much.

Two years ago I went on this Buddhist retreat with my Mum. She is a member of a Sangha [Buddhist community]. At the retreat, a lady monk there was about fifty years old but she had no wrinkles! It's just right living I think. Buddhist precepts are a guide for living. Through my Mum, I have been exposed to the writings of Thich Nhat Hanh, who is an internationally renowned Buddhist author. I like going with Mum to the meditations at the Sangha because they always have these really interesting talks. I like the meditation part because I find we never really stop and meditating forces you to!

If more people meditated it would help with a lot of things in society such as depression. It also would help for any grieving process.

Living is very different from existing! But there are few role models to show the way of how to be happy. I appreciate different qualities and strengths in people, but I haven't seen it all wrapped up in one package yet!

But it's all a part and a symptom of the number one problem for girls – which is that all girls think they have to be beautiful. There's this impression among girls that you can be the most successful person in the world, but if you're ugly, no one will care.

I had a really bad year in 2002 - I call it my annus horribilus - when my parents split up, a friend of mine died, another friend's father died, there were car accidents and I had an accident too. It was a weird, terrible year. Sometimes I wonder if it was astrological. But I know that no matter how bad things seemed at the time, I knew eventually I would come through it.

I have experienced depression, although I have never really talked about it much. At one point I got so sad that I stopped talking. You can't grasp something unless you've been through it really, and no one else can take away the problem for you. It's healthier if you can unload and talk about things. Sometimes the only thing that works is time. Now I'm so much happier because I have achieved all that I wanted to and I don't feel as pressured about things.

I've come through a lot. At a party at the end of [illegible] a bottle [illegible] aimed at someone else [illegible] sudden and massive impact and at [illegible] seemed to fracture [illegible] bottle hit my mouth [illegible] ll [illegible] out of my mouth [illegible] out. The [illegible] people at the party [illegible] People went silent. I didn't cry. I stood up - I was in shock - and all I could manage was, "Could someone please call an ambulance?" The boys were stoked and they were like, "She's taking it like a man!!" The girls couldn't look. I was lucky that I had just turned my head at the precise second of impact, because it didn't hit a nerve. I never found out who did it. I went to school without any teeth for a week! **I realized as a result of being hurt that people did care about me. When it happened I lost some of my faith in human nature, but the way people responded gave me hope again.** Everyone was really kind. Now I see the accident as almost a good thing!

After that, I became ill with glandular fever. It must have been due to all the stress from that year - but I got through it. I think I just needed a break that summer so I got glandular fever and put myself to bed for nine weeks. I'm lucky with my parents because they are both so understanding - my Mum is a really talented fabric painter and my father is a writer and has been a journalist - so they have cared for me and supported me throughout everything and in all my endeavors and dreams. And I'm also really lucky to have two best friends, Sari and April, who are such good friends to me. They're always there for me!

My favorite book is by the Indian writer Rohinton Mistry, *A Fine Balance*. Maybe there is some kind of significance in that! I don't know … My dream for the future is to become a foreign correspondent. I want to travel the world and write. I couldn't think of anything better.

The first five seconds of meeting someone most people have already decided whether the other person is good looking or not. That's basically how most people think. But what relevance does being good looking have to anything?!

07
RGS
NAME: JENNIFER MARCOTTE
D.O.B: 26.09.80
AGE: 24 YEARS OLD
NATIONALITY: CANADIAN
LIVES: TORQUAY, SASKATCHEWAN
OCCUPATION: TRAVELER / WAITRESS / SALES REP

I NEVER DO WHAT ANYONE THINKS I'M GOING TO DO. ONCE I MAKE A DECISION TO DO SOMETHING, I NEVER BACK OUT.

HER STORY:

I met Jennifer when I saw her outside my living room window, a long way from her native Canada. She was standing on the street and even from a distance it was obvious she was upset. I wandered out to see if she was in need of any assistance. Jennifer ended up coming into my place for a cup of tea. It turned out she had just broken up with her boyfriend and he had driven off, leaving her by herself. After briefly telling me the story, she composed herself and we ended up laughing about the crazy situations you can get yourself into over love and relationships. Over the course of the next few months I had the pleasure of getting to know her, while she was holidaying in my area.

Jennifer calls herself "just a farm girl", and her dream job would be to be a Recruit Trainer for the Royal Canadian Mountain Police. Jennifer is a very determined person - she has no fear about risks, nor of taking on a challenge. Naturally fit and with a love of doing physical things, she is a feisty and energetic individual, who loves exhausting herself. She is also intelligent and opinionated and she carries herself with grace.

I was born in Canada, in the small town of Torquay in the province of Saskatchewan. Torquay is a small country town, there are only a few hundred people living there. I am the second youngest of four girls. My sisters and I all look alike. When we were younger there was quite a bit of sibling rivalry. That is not so much the case any more. Now nobody could tell whether we are friends or sisters. We're all different and we're all right, all the time! The arguments in our house are interesting - sometimes they're over nothing. [laughs] My poor Dad - he has to deal with these five women [including my Mom]. We can get into it sometimes! My sister, who is the eldest, will always be saying, "Can't we all get along?" and we're all yelling back at her, "But we're fighting!". [laughs] It can be crazy.

My parents have been married for approximately thirty years. They are so peaceful! I have never heard my parents yell at each other. They don't fight really. My Mom is so young and energetic. She's always busy. My father loves children so he just takes it all in his stride. There is nothing he likes better than children. But he's needed to become patient - he never used to be - there were five girls and one bathroom! I get along really well with my father. I'm really punctual. I'm never late. And so is he … not like some of my other sisters and my Mom!

I am a farm girl. Really! I am SUCH a farm girl and it's becoming more and more apparent that I am a farm girl - take it or leave it! [laughs] I could drive a thirty-two gear tractor when I was twelve years old. I used to do babysitting at the same age for [Canadian]$2 an hour. I learned the value of money early. I once ran up a $480 phone bill and my parents made me pay it back out of my two dollars-per-hour babysitting money! I'm so grateful to my parents though. Now I never spend money I don't have. It was a good lesson.

At school I never did rough copies of my homework, I only did one copy. **I make the good one the first time. I BELIEVE THAT IF YOU ARE GOING TO DO IT, YOU SHOULD DO IT RIGHT THE FIRST TIME. I NEVER GOT FULL MARKS BUT I ALWAYS DID WELL.** I attended a local high school. I wasn't "cool" when I was in school — I was always different. At first it was me not fitting in, and then it was me choosing to be different. I am my Mom's wild child! She calls me her spunky, wilful child!

There were only eight people in my graduation class. They were really intelligent and talented people. They could all sing and act, they were sporty and artistic, but many of them didn't try. I wasn't the smartest, but I was on the honor roll when I graduated. I see them on the odd occasion. Much as I love them as brothers and sisters - I didn't bond on the level they bonded. They were all drinkers. I was never a drinker. Some kids used to come to school drunk! They had all this talent and they wasted it on drinking. It's such a waste! I have never drunk alcohol or tried drugs in my life.

ALCOHOL IN SMALL TOWNS IS ALWAYS A PROBLEM. BUT IF ANY OF THEM EVER NEEDED ME I'D BE THERE. I care about them but I don't have the urge to keep in touch all the time.

Traveling as a backpacker has been such a radical education for me. There have been times when I hated it, and couldn't wait to get home. But at other times the experiences have just been a revelation. When I decided to go away, no one believed me! I never do what anyone thinks I'm going to do. It took me a while to make the decision, but once I decide, I never back out!

I have learned a lot about myself - not necessarily all good either!

If you're going to do
something, do it right
the first time!

And I have learned about others too. I have seen and met a lot of girls from all over on my travels. **THE NUMBER ONE ISSUE AS I SEE IT FOR YOUNG WOMEN IS THAT THEY CARE TOO MUCH ABOUT THEIR WEIGHT AND NOT ENOUGH ABOUT THEIR HEALTH.** They eat the wrong things endlessly, or it seems that they don't eat at all. It's not just the relationship to food either, it's the obsessive mindset and the lack of self-value. They don't seem to value themselves over the image of what they are striving for. They don't look in the mirror and ask, "What do I want for myself?" They look and wonder, "What do other people think?" **They don't think for themselves.**

The most anorexic person I have seen since I've been away from home was another backpacker — her bones were sticking out of her skin. She was obviously really unwell. I felt so sorry for her. There is a difference between someone who is naturally skinny and someone who has their bones sticking out. I don't understand it but there is obviously a point where they can't see it any more. They have started the weight loss to attract guys or to be beautiful, but then they've gone too far the other way. It's really sad.

If only more girls would get into fitness - I mean really get into it as a way of life! Fitness is really important.

I'm not sure what I would study if I were to again. I never really wanted to go to university, because I was never really sure what I wanted. It has to really interest me. Otherwise I won't try. I definitely want to learn about nutrition and my dream job is to join the Royal Canadian Mountain Police. I wanted to join before I went traveling and I already passed the entrance exam. It's a big process to get in, just to get into the course is a big process. When I get back to Canada, I'm having an interview. Eventually I would love to be the trainer of the new recruits, or be responsible for anything involving fitness and endurance.

I have been around horses since I can remember, they have featured in my whole life. I grew up horseback riding. My fiancé was a cowboy who used to ride bareback in the rodeo and he used to train horses. One memory I have is when my Dad sold my horse to the glue factory - to the hackers. I was absolutely distraught. But it had to be done 'cos he was sick and had foundered. His name was "Bandit". I wasn't meant to know but then I saw my horse in the trailer and Dad was saying to me, "Jen, it has to be done". I understood though. But my Dad had put it off for ages and he was thinking more of my feelings not his pocketbook. He was more concerned about my loss. I was really sad.

I have been sad a lot in my life too. I was manic depressive when I was in my teens, around the age of fourteen or fifteen. At that time, one of the few people I could talk to was my uncle, my father's brother. He died of cancer and that was hard for me to deal with. He was always very kind to me. He made me feel very special. I was always quite over-emotional when I was younger, but I wouldn't go to a doctor or a psychiatrist, even though my Mom wanted me to. But we were quite poor, I didn't come from a wealthy family and my Mom worked. I used to think that people were always talking about me! I was just scared though. I thought I was being criticized. I was bullied at school a lot, from the ages of seven to nine. I had really long hair and I got picked on. It was jealousy too. In the end it was okay, everyone grows up and children can be so cruel. But when I see or experience any kind of bullying I still get upset. But I now know that it's not my problem. It's always someone else's insecurity.

I HAD A REALLY GOOD FAMILY. I WAS SO LUCKY! BUT ALL THOSE YEARS I DIDN'T KNOW. I JUST FELT ATTACKED AND HAD NO DEFENSE.

I tend to go into something one hundred and ten percent! Instead of starting a relationship and just going through the process naturally and at a reasonable pace, I tend to go very deep, very fast. In the past I have transferred love from one relationship to the next, which isn't a good idea! I have been engaged before. I jumped in too deep and he went too, which was crazy. He just went with it, even though he really wasn't the guy for me. We decided to get married when I was sixteen! So we broke up. In hindsight I wasn't meant to be with him, because I would have been eternally naive and over-protected. I would never have been able to do something for myself. The next relationship wasn't right either. He actually hit me and was abusive. But I couldn't let go of the need for that intensity, which I had basically carried over from my engagement. I was attempting to recreate my previous relationship. But I worked that out soon enough and broke it off. **It was another good lesson!**

I'm looking for one person. That's it. I want one person who I love so much and who loves me the same. If they died, then for me, that would be it. I wouldn't need anyone else after experiencing that kind of love I don't think. How do you start over again? I think it would take years to get over that kind of loss. I believe everyone is meant to do something different and that I'll know it when I meet the person who is for me.

This trip has been good for me on so many levels. It's put everything into perspective for me. I could truly see anyone from my past and be cool with them. **BUT I'M DONE WITH ANALYZING MY LIFE. NOW I JUST WANT TO GET ON WITH IT.**

08
RGS

NAME: SEE DEWI WIMALADHARMA
D.O.B: 13.09.78
AGE: 25 YEARS OLD
NATIONALITY: SRI LANKAN
LIVES: DAMBULLAH
OCCUPATION: BATIK FACTORY MANAGER

See Dewi runs a batik factory in the Dambullah area, a few hours from the capital, Colombo, in Sri Lanka. The business, "Henry Batiks", is family-owned and was handed down from her Sinhalese grandfather to her father. The torch is now being passed to See Dewi, who has been working in the craft-based textile business since 1994. A shy yet warm young woman, See Dewi radiates a gentle presence and a quiet determination to take on more responsibility in her father's business until she can start a new business of her own. A devout Buddhist and wife to Sagara, whom she married in 1997, See Dewi is also the proud mother of two-year-old Uvindu. I met See Dewi when I was traveling in Sri Lanka. I spotted her brightly colored batiks hanging out the front of her shop while driving on the Kandy Road, en route to the Buddhist center and major trading town of Kandy, and I pulled over to buy some. See Dewi was one of the first REAL GIRLS I interviewed for this book.

Be happy with what you have, you have enough!

I am the manager here now, but the business was begun by my grandfather and he then handed it to my father, who went into the business when he was twenty-five. I started in the factory when I was fourteen years old, in 1994. We have about ten people who work here, plus the family. **We all work around here!**

The first thing, it was the learning part - you know? I had to learn everything about the cloth, how to do batches, the dye lots, what the process of making batik was. Then I had to learn how to explain it to the customers who came in from the road. I used to take them around the factory showing them how the fabric is produced, and how we do the designs because it is such a traditional fabric and it's all done by hand here. From there I learned the sales side. And I used to just help out in the shop, because I liked it, as **a hobby and now it's a career.** It was just fun really. It still is!

I finished high school, to what we call here, "all levels". After graduating I was made the manager of the two shops by my father.

I want to help my father until I am able to start my own batik clothing business. I want to go to Kandy [an important trading town several hours away] because my husband, Sagara, lives there during the week. He works in a garment factory there. He's learning the manufacturing of painted batik-cloth blouses so I can supply my father's shops with batik clothing. We eventually want to have our own batik shop in Kandy. Here is the beginning of my sample range. I hope people like them!

My son is two years old. His name is Uvindu Huryjith Wimaladharma. I would like to have one more child, maybe next year. My parents and my brother are very supportive and they can help me to manage the factory if I need help.

In the morning we wash at around 11 o'clock to midday. **Then we make pujas, which are flowers and offerings for the Gods.** Once we have made our pujas, we go into the meditation room and pray before Buddha. Then we have our main meal of the day. If someone's sick or we want to protect a baby we do patini, a special cleansing ritual in the morning and in the afternoon. In the evenings we make hot tea for the Gods to safeguard the business. The Gods we worship and make offerings to include Lakshmi [Hindu Goddess of wealth and prosperity], Vishnu [Hindu God of "right action" and goodness], Ganesh [Hindu God of worldly fulfillment] and the Goddess of Katharagama, [Valli Ama, consort of Skanda] for the blessing unions. When I make my own house I am going to have one special room for making rituals and pujas.

My son makes me very happy. I just want to grow him up properly and teach him everything! I want to have a good solid family with my husband. Relationships and family are the most important things in life.

I FELT THAT I WAS NOT JUST SOMEONE'S DAUGHTER, WIFE, SISTER OR MOTHER. JUST MYSELF. IT WAS A BIG MOMENT.

We are living a long way from it [the fighting in the north of the country], but I would like it if my son goes into the defense forces. It would be something that he can do if he wants to, a job for his family and for his country, for Sri Lankans.

When he is old enough I would tell him that he can stand on his own and not to "use" other people. **I would tell him, "Don't hate other people, make your own effort, rely on yourself – you can do it on your own".**

My advice would be not to cause any problems for other people. When you have or when you do something of your own or you "carry" yourself. You are responsible for your life and you are not needing others to "carry" you. And when you have something, think to yourself "I have enough". Be happy with what you have, you have enough! Don't be envious of others, it's not good to be jealous of someone who has more than you do - be happy that they've come up [got ahead] in life.

We pray to God [Buddha] and then he helps us with any problems. Buddha is the one I really look up to. But it's everyone's choice to pray to whom they want. You can pray to Sai Baba or another guru, whomever you want, but no human can replace the Supreme Being, that is the Buddha, for me.

I went to a Catholic School so when I am in Colombo [the capital of Sri Lanka]I also go to church to attend Mass, and I go to the local kovil [temple] once a month. I pray to protect my family and my baby and I pray to achieve ascension or enlightenment. This is what we aim for - and we believe our next life depends on this too - and so that is what we do in this lifetime to influence that, we pray to become enlightened.

In 2001, I went to Europe with my husband, my brother and three friends of my brother. We went to Lourdes in France - the sacred place for Catholics all over the world - as I had wanted to go there all my life. We visited Germany, France, Monaco, Italy.

Going to Lourdes was a dream of mine. It's a very beautiful church and I had wanted to see it for myself, because I had learned about it when I was still at school. I was so happy to go there, and I got holy water! I want to go back there and so the next time I have some money, I will go again.

When I was at Lourdes I saw lots of sick people who went there to be healed by the holy water. There were people in wheelchairs everywhere - I saw so many! For some reason I was very sad, and even though I was with a group too, I felt very alone. I felt that I wanted to stay there forever and not come home to Sri Lanka. It was the first time that I had a **strong sense of myself** as a person, as an individual.

NOTE: **The Sinhalese or Sri Lankan form of Buddhism is very influenced by Hinduism, due to the proximity and the relationship of Sri Lanka to India. Buddhism is understood to have derived originally from Hinduism and the Buddha was but one of the Gods that were prayed to. In Sri Lanka, the Buddha is the primary God in prayers and rituals, although the other deities are still tremendously important and continue to be worshiped daily.**

At the time I met See Dewi in August 2002, a temporary ceasefire had been called in the nearly thirty-year war that had been raging in Sri Lanka. **The intense fighting between the Sri Lankan Army and the Sri Lankan rebel forces of the LTTE - or the "Tamil Tigers" as they are more known - was put on official hold pending the outcome of the peace talks. The peace talks were hailed as a major breakthrough in an entrenched civil war that had divided the country, claiming hundreds of thousands of lives and effectively isolating Sri Lanka from the rest of the world. For the millions displaced by the war, the ceasefire offered the prospect of finally being able to return to their homes. Against this backdrop of national and international hopes for a lasting peace, an ongoing controversy was the mounting evidence presented by aid agencies of child soldiers being conscripted on both sides of the war - a charge that was being denied by the Sri Lankan government

I've only been in Auckland a short time. I came from Christchurch originally, so I'm still getting used to things. **My parents are Christian. They have been a huge influence on me.** I was brought up a Christian from day dot! We went to church every week. My father works at a paper mill and my mother is a teacher. Currently she isn't teaching. She is a chaplain at a local high school. It was always an open-door policy at our house. I have an older sister. She and I are close. My parents often had a lot of people staying. If anyone in the neighborhood needed help, my parents would help them. We often didn't know how many people would be at the dinner table! They have amazing hearts. **I went to film school but currently I work as a fundraiser** and I do fundraising events for the International Red Cross for the New Zealand branch, to go towards their needs in the war zones of the world. Very specialized people go into the war zones – I've never been – you have to be able to handle it so only special people go overseas and do that. **It's a huge thing to be put on them psychologically. I would like to go into a war zone but I know that at the moment I wouldn't be able to handle it.** I know that I can do my work and raising funds for the war zones is what I can do. New Zealand is a rich country and we have the resources but I'm happy to be

NAME: SUSI FOOKES
D.O.B: 25.09.79
AGE: 25 YEARS OLD
NATIONALITY: NEW ZEALANDER
LIVES: AUCKLAND, NEW ZEALAND
OCCUPATION: FUNDRAISER FOR THE INTERNATIONAL RED CROSS SOCIETY

HER STORY:

I found Susi leaning against a long settee in a darkened rosy-hued nightclub in Auckland. She looked other-worldly, bathed in the red light from the internal decorations of the club's lounge bar. In sharp contrast to other club patrons, she wasn't even drinking. Instead she was sitting perfectly still - resting actually - while people swirled around her, buzzing in and out of the loud gig that was on in the room behind. She looked as calm and peaceful as anyone you would expect to find in a monastery. There was this aura about her. She looked like an angel! And as it turns out, so she is. Susi works full-time for the Red Cross and is responsible for fundraising for the New Zealand branch. An inspiring person with a huge heart, Susi is a shining example of how to contribute to society and remain fiercely individual.

EVENTUALLY I WOULD REALLY LOVE TO WRITE ILLUSTRATED CHILDREN'S BOOKS.

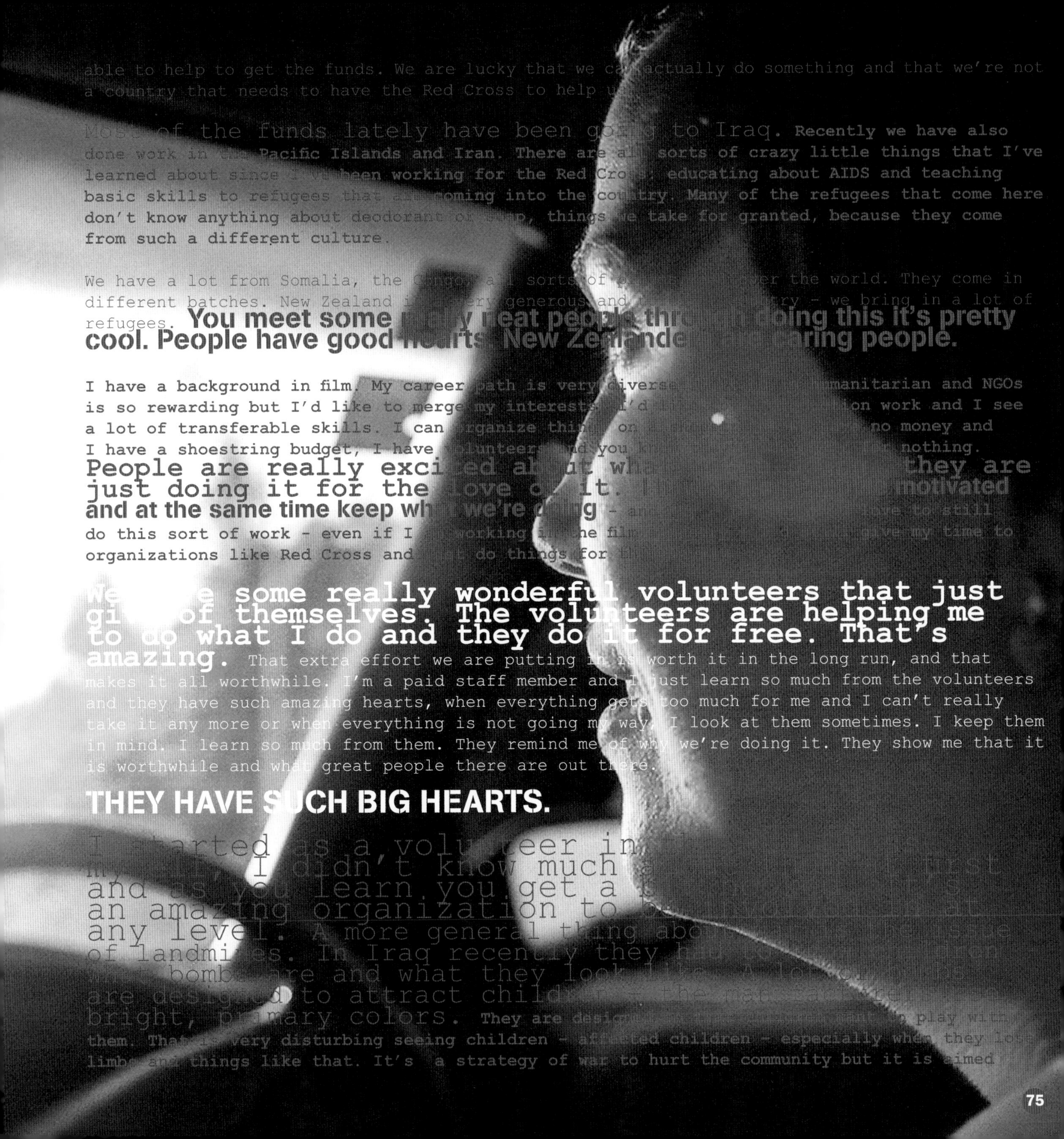

able to help to get the funds. We are lucky that we can actually do something and that we're not a country that needs to have the Red Cross to help us.

Most of the funds lately have been going to Iraq. Recently we have also done work in the Pacific Islands and Iran. There are all sorts of crazy little things that I've learned about since I've been working for the Red Cross: educating about AIDS and teaching basic skills to refugees that are coming into the country. Many of the refugees that come here don't know anything about deodorant or soap, things we take for granted, because they come from such a different culture.

We have a lot from Somalia, the Congo, all sorts of [illegible] over the world. They come in different batches. New Zealand is a very generous and [illegible] country – we bring in a lot of refugees. **You meet some [illegible] neat people thro[illegible] doing this it's pretty cool. People have good hearts. New Zealande[illegible] caring people.**

I have a background in film. My career path is very diverse [illegible] humanitarian and NGOs is so rewarding but I'd like to merge my interests. I'd [illegible] on work and I see a lot of transferable skills. I can organize thin[illegible] on [illegible] no money and I have a shoestring budget, I have volunteers and you kn[illegible] nothing. **People are really exci[illegible] ab[illegible] wh[illegible] they are just doing it for the love of it. I [illegible] motivated and at the same time keep wh[illegible] we're doing** – an[illegible] love to still do this sort of work – even if I [illegible] working in the film [illegible] give my time to organizations like Red Cross and [illegible] do things for th[illegible]

We have some really wonderful volunteers that just give of themselves. The volunteers are helping me to do what I do and they do it for free. That's amazing. That extra effort we are putting in is worth it in the long run, and that makes it all worthwhile. I'm a paid staff member and I just learn so much from the volunteers and they have such amazing hearts, when everything gets too much for me and I can't really take it any more or when everything is not going my way, I look at them sometimes. I keep them in mind. I learn so much from them. They remind me of why we're doing it. They show me that it is worthwhile and what great people there are out there.

THEY HAVE SUCH BIG HEARTS.

I started as a volunteer in [illegible] my [illegible], I didn't know much [illegible] first and as you learn you get a [illegible] an amazing organization to [illegible] any level. A more general thing abo[illegible] of landmines. In Iraq recently they ha[illegible] what bombs are and what they look like. A lot of [illegible] are designed to attract children – the manufacturers [illegible] bright, primary colors. They are design[illegible] play with them. That is very disturbing seeing children – affected children – especially when they lose limbs and things like that. It's a strategy of war to hurt the community but it is aimed [illegible] specifically at children. That for me is the hardest thing. It's harder for me than when an adult is hurt. I mean I don't like it when anyone gets hurt, but I especially don't like hearing the stories about children being hurt or maimed.

I WOULDN'T KNOW WHAT TO SAY TO THOSE LEADERS AND THE TERRORISTS RESPONSIBLE for the children who have been hurt or killed. It's just not right though. How do they sleep? If that was their children … what would they think? The damage is irreversible and it ruins lives.

I've seen photos from Iraq. The places they were hiding the bombs and ammunition were schools and places like that. But kids are kids and they're going to get into stuff. **IT'S NOT COOL.**

Working in a humanitarian organization, I've obviously seen the worst of human nature, but I've also met some amazing people too, I've seen the best and the worst of humanity through my work. It's kind of given me hope really!

WE SHOULD JUST BE HAPPY WITH OUR CIRCUMSTANCES. THAT'S WHAT MY NANA TAUGHT ME. SHE DIED RECENTLY AND ALL SHE USED TO ASK ME WAS "BUT ARE YOU HAPPY?" THAT'S ALL SHE CARED ABOUT AND SHE WAS RIGHT. THE MOST IMPORTANT THING IS TO BE HAPPY.

IT WOULD BE REALLY GOOD FOR YOUNG GIRLS TO GET INVOLVED IN NGOs AND HUMANITARIAN ORGANIZATIONS – IT WOULD TAKE THEIR MIND OFF THE MORE SUPERFICIAL ASPECTS OF LIFE. I have a volunteer at the moment who's doing work experience with me, and she left school at thirteen. She came to work for me and now she's sixteen and it has definitely changed her, she's quite a different person now. I try to give her lots of praise and keep her motivated. I love telling her stories, to see her reaction to things, I've seen her commitment to the job grow. I can see her think about things, she is thinking about the bigger picture now which is amazing. It can change your life and change your outlook. It's changed mine.

In New Zealand we have only seen Red Cross in action in World War II, therefore we don't yet have the younger generation as involved. It's because we don't know about war, we are so blessed but that's the reason we should be giving, **we are the ones who should be so grateful and who can afford to give.**

OUR GENERATION DOESN'T KNOW WE'RE ALIVE! WE HAVEN'T SEEN WAR. WE HAVE NEVER REALLY SEEN POVERTY. WE ARE SO LUCKY.

NAME: ALISON CULPIN

OCCUPATION: DEMOGRAPHER

10 RGS

HER STORY:

Alison Culpin is many things. She is driven. She is extreme. She is disciplined. She is tough, a word she uses a lot. For a couple of years before I eventually met her through a mutual friend, I had heard about Alison's magnificent obsession: endurance- and terrain-based mountain bike riding in extreme conditions. By that time she had ended her quest to win one of the toughest terrain bike races in the world, The Simpson Desert Cycle Challenge.

Alison is that rare individual, a quiet and almost painfully shy person who prefers her actions - and in particular her riding skills - to speak for her. But the lovely thing about such inscrutability is that when she finally opens up, she's got a lot to say: About how a person can traverse over one thousand sand dunes and stay sane. About what goes on in your mind when the outside temperature hits fifty degrees celsius [a hundred and twenty-two degrees farenheit] and there is no shade for one hundred kilometers. About how to find yourself and lose your ego – all the while holding on to your willpower to keep moving forward. About what happens when you put your self willingly through mental and physical hell, not once but several times.

Alison Culpin is truly remarkable.

ENDURANCE RACING HAS MADE ME MORE SELF-AWARE. IT HAS ENCOURAGED ME TO DO MORE THINGS, TO TAKE MORE RISKS IN LIFE IN GENERAL, NOT JUST IN THE PHYSICAL SENSE.

I study the population, using forecasting or projection techniques. I look at the movements or shifts. Because I work for the Department of Education, I use the information and my projections to work out where new schools can be planned. We call these "school catchments".

THE POPULATION ISSUE IS GOING TO BE THE GLOBAL ISSUE FOR THE FUTURE. Large families will probably be a thing of the past in even fifty years. The planet can't sustain infinite population growth. And everyone should become much more aware of that. Education is the most important thing.

There is no official population policy in Australia. The only thing that comes close is the annual target for migration. In a country like Australia, it's pretty hard to have controls over fertility or mortality, however if it weren't for migration we would actually have a declining population. One of the things that the media always reports is that we need immigration because of the declining population, but that's false demographically. If we had one hundred and fifty thousand in net immigration, the average age of the Australian population would decrease by only half a year, because we are bringing in mostly older people. We need to bring in babies to really make a difference to the average age of our population!

I do have concerns about overcrowding, destruction of the environment, just being able to swim anywhere. We have a tiny rim of coastal environment where almost everybody lives. However, it's being over-used and over-developed.

I will most likely be "the one" of the statistically one in four people who won't have children. Anyway, I can't see it… yet!

I grew up in Sydney's Lane Cove area near the Lane Cove River, where there was a lot of open space to muck around and I was always athletic and into sports. I started off doing triathlons – a swim, bike and run – but then that got a bit boring. I enjoyed the challenge and initially I wasn't obsessive about it. That came later! It started off being really fun – and although I was competitive, I didn't want to specialize in triathlons. One of the main things that put me off was the level of pretentiousness that crept into the events – having to have the right gear and so on. All of a sudden money or being seen to have money was important. And the people mix had gradually changed. I wanted to get back to grassroots and I wanted to focus more on bike riding because that was my strength.

I SUPPOSE I GOT HOOKED ON THE ENDORPHIN RUSH THAT YOU GET FROM ENDURANCE RACING! I first heard about the Simpson Desert Cycle Challenge [SDCC] about three or four years before I actually went in it. I found out about it through an article in a cycling magazine. But really for me at the time, it wasn't even a goal. It was nothing that definite, it was just sitting there in the back of my mind festering away! I just thought to myself, "One day …" The Simpson Desert Cycle Challenge is one of the most radical – extreme – mountain bike races in the world. It's got a reputation. It's a physical and a mental challenge. So you have to be ready for it. It's not something you do frivolously. I learned that because I was seriously under-prepared the first time!

In 1998, I had the opportunity to have a support crew – **it is vital to have a support crew.** It generally consists of two people, plus a four-wheel-drive vehicle, water and supplies. And it's camping the whole time. You have to bring everything you need for a whole week plus backup supplies in case you get stuck somewhere.

THE RACE CONSISTS OF ELEVEN HUNDRED SAND DUNES and it COVERS FIVE HUNDRED AND EIGHTY-THREE KILOMETERS IN TOTAL

[three hundred and sixty five miles] from Purnie Bore to the small outback town of Birdsville. So it's way way out there! The course is terrain – not bitumen – consisting of sand corrugations [ridges caused by the winds] and dirt. The race proceeds go to a really good cause: the sole beneficiary is the Paraplegic Benefit Fund of Australia.

You drive out to this little place called Purnie Bore. It's nothing but a little lake in the middle of nowhere! I had no idea what to expect. I had never even spoken to anybody about the race! I think my aunt and uncle had a better understanding about it than I did. [laughs] I got the race booklet with my registration and that was the sum total of my research. Actually it was a good thing because **had I known how bad it was going to be that first year, I'd never have done it in the first place.**

The idea is that the rider who does the best time in and finishes each of the sections before the sweep vehicle comes in [you have to beat the sweep vehicle otherwise you don't finish the section], is the overall winner. There is a men's and a women's division. Only a handful of riders, the elite endurance riders, will finish every section over the five days. **BUT THAT'S WHAT YOU HAVE TO DO TO WIN.**

At night you set up camp. And then it's rest, repair, recover, eat, drink. During the race I drink about sixteen to eighteen liters of water a day. One of my earliest challenges – trying to find a place to go to the toilet! The first time I went about fifty meters off to the side of the track, but by the third day I was just squatting in the middle of the track. There is no time for the niceties.

I have entered the race three times. I was all lined up to go in 1999, but two days before leaving, I fell off my bike and broke my shoulder. It was fairly major because I ended up in hospital and had a rehabilitation period of about four months. I had a few reactions to that. I was upset. I was disappointed. I was really sad that I was missing it. Most of all I was annoyed that I had to stay home. I might go back this year in October.

It's rugged! It's called the Rig Road, but it's a dirt and sand track basically. **The first year, I lost all feeling in my left hand from the sand corrugations.** The vibrations went through the handlebars on my bike into my hands and just numbed my left hand completely! I didn't get the feeling back for about a week afterwards.

The temperature gets up to fifty degrees celsius [a hundred and twenty-two degrees farenheit] on the track. People drop out of the race all the time when it gets too much to take. About thirty to forty people go in the race, but when the conditions get too hard, only about a handful will complete the course.

When you see the sweep vehicle and you're pushing your bike through a tough bit, you start running even though, once you're in that situation, you rarely have a chance to beat it! I remember looking over my shoulder and it was just this overwhelming feeling of disappointment. I was shattered because I knew I wasn't going to finish.

I just couldn't believe how much sand there was! I imagined going out there and I'd be racing against other people, but it's mostly just you … and limitless amounts of sand. You just look to the horizon and see this narrow little sliver of yellow up to the sky and occasionally you'll see a little dot on it – which is another competitor – to reassure you that you're on the right track. A couple of people – guys actually – freaked out in the isolation. One guy wouldn't ride by himself – he was terrified.

I found the solitary nature of the event one of the better parts of the experience. I found I enjoyed being out there, just doing my own thing. Lots of times I wanted to stop but it was so hot and disgusting and there was no shade, so stopping would have been worse! On one occasion one of the guys couldn't go any further. He ended up digging a little hole on the sand dune and covering himself in sand, trying to get some relief. People have some wild experiences during the race.

FIND AN
ACTIVITY THAT
YOU LOVE TO
DO AND STICK
AT IT

There is mostly a whole lot of arguing in my head, back and forth, like "You're never coming out here again – remember how horrible it is!" LOTS OF SWEARING IN THERE! But then the steely determination sets in with, "Don't let the bastard sweep catch you!"[laughs] A lot of it was pride. Often I'd be in tears, generally in the afternoon sections. That was usually the point when I'd be the most mentally and physically depleted. There were often times when everything was rock bottom. And naturally that would be the exact moment you'd hit a series of sand dunes, when you have no option but to push the bike through miles of sand just to get through to a rideable section. There's sand in your shoes, flies all over your face and the sun hitting the backs of your legs.

The worst bits – the times when I really struggle – always happen out on the track. But the first time I got "swept" in 1998, **I BURST INTO TEARS** when I finally arrived at the campsite. That was partly because I felt like I'd be letting people down – in that case my aunt and uncle who were my support crew – and also because I hadn't finished the section. I had gone out there not even imagining that I wouldn't finish the race, **I had not prepared myself for any sort of disaster or letdown.** I am fairly hard on myself though. I have high standards for myself in certain things. I can be very dedicated in certain things and at the same time let other things drift along.

But I always try to keep in mind that I willingly put myself there. The extreme lows are nothing compared to the extreme highs. It is a roller coaster emotionally, all day for five days. But at the end of it you feel amazing, it's as though you've gone through some bizarre initiation process. There is this incredible sense of achievement, just to have survived the ordeal. The benefit for me is being more relaxed when I come back to my normal life. I don't get as worked up about the little things. It's a big release.

I can always think to myself during the non-race times in my life, **"No matter how tough it gets, it will never be as tough as that".**

The first time I attempted the race in 1998, I made eight out of the nine sections, and came seventeenth overall out of a total of thirty-four riders. I came second out of the three women in the race. In 2000, I came seventeenth again, but this time out of a total of fifty-four riders! And I was first out of the two women. And then in 2001, I finished all nine sections for the first time. That was the year I got my hundred percent! That was when I went, "Ok, I've reached my goal". **Now, the next time I go in it, it can be to have fun and to see my friends!**

Another good thing I did get out of it – and this has nothing to do with the actual riding – is **THE APPRECIATION I NOW HAVE FOR A WIDE VARIETY OF PEOPLE.** Such characters go riding! And the party at the end of the race at the famous Birdsville Pub is massive. Mostly the support crews hang out late, the riders are always in bed by 9pm!

But then there are other good things … the outback is a different kind of environmental beauty. I had always been a coastal, beach-oriented person before.

I have been single for about a year. My former partner was also a rider, but he's pretty much given up riding and is pursuing other things. But I'm not ready to give it up yet. I have one brother who's a couple of years older. He thinks I'm mad! I think he's a bit proud, but he still shakes his head about it all! My parents don't really like me being out on the bike all the time, mainly because of the dangers on the roads when I'm training. And they are probably just sick of hearing about the Simpson Desert!

I think I would be the most persistent extreme mountain bike rider. I am by no means the most talented, put I'm perhaps the most dogged.

I am not the most confident person. I'm not really "out there", but **WHEN I'M ON THE BIKE, TRAINING AND COMPETING, I DO BECOME THIS VERY SELF-CONTAINED, FOCUSED AND DETERMINED PERSON. I GUESS I FEEL IN CONTROL OF THINGS.**

Not that I don't get scared before a race though! I'm always nervous. Every single day of the race I'm a bundle of nerves, but I figure a little bit is good. It gets everything revved up. I also look at everyone else and realize that there is most likely going to be someone worse off than me. Once the race starts though, all that becomes irrelevant. Once you're doing what you're there to do, the fear leaves the body.

ENDURANCE RACING HAS MADE ME MORE SELF-AWARE. It has encouraged me to do more things, to take more risks in life in general, not just in the physical sense.

I'm going to do a team adventure race. There is one that is similar to an eco-challenge, but it's only a three-day event. It's a mixture of mountain biking, trekking, kayaking and snorkeling. It should be interesting – there are underwater checkpoints. And there is the Central Australia Bike Challenge, which I would really like to do. It's technically a hard race as it's very rocky terrain, but the race is more luxurious – you stay in hotel rooms, so you've got bathrooms!

11
RGS
NAME/S: VITHYA BERNARD REVAL
& GNANAPRAGA
O.B: 06.02 & 05.09.8
GE: 21 & 2 YEARS OLD
ATIONALITY: SRI LANKAN
IVES: JAFFNA, NORTHERN SRI LANKA
CCUPATION: BIOSCIENCE STUDENTS

THEIR STORIES:

I met these two remarkable young women while traveling in the north of Sri Lanka. I had been keen to go to the north of the country for a long time and, with the announcement of the ceasefire in the Sri Lankan civil war, I jumped at the chance. Cut off from the rest of the country by the ominous Elephant Pass, Jaffna is at the end of the narrow archipelago that separates this stronghold LTTE / Tamil Tiger occupied territory from the rest of Sri Lanka. The area has been the focus of the very worst of the fighting and has been inaccessible to all but aid agencies for the better part of three decades. After weighing the odds and consulting with some of the travel guides who had returned from the north, I decided to go anyway. At one checkpoint along the way I was warned by the aid workers manning the Red Cross booth not to go to Jaffna, but certainly not to walk anywhere until we got into Jaffna itself, due to the enormous number of landmines buried everywhere else. Six checkpoints later and just when I was beginning to get nervous, I was richly rewarded for the effort, and for that I have to thank my amazing Sinhalese driver Siri, who made the trip possible.

Not surprisingly, the roads into Jaffna reveal roadside houses as a **mess of blackened and crumbling ruins.** Any structure that hasn't been completely destroyed by the relentless shelling has been well marked by gunfire and shrapnel. The town square however, looked like business as usual when we arrived. According to the shopkeepers the market was just starting to show signs of almost bustling life again. There was a sort of wary optimism in the streets generally. Meanwhile, the army was out and about, using the ceasefire as an opportunity to roll out yet more barbed wire and shore up the many wooden and green-sandbagged bunkers that were in the middle of the streets, in trees, in empty lots and basically everywhere you looked.

We could find nowhere to stay: the one or two guesthouses that were listed in the guide were full of mostly Western aid workers and the odd Sri Lankan family whose house had been destroyed in the fighting. Eventually, the intrepid Siri - who is Sinhalese and therefore a potential target for rogue Tamil soldiers - cleverly selected the Catholic part of town to ask for help, which arrived in the form of a shopkeeper who allowed us to stay in his home. We discovered that to cope financially, many people in the area had converted their homes into boarding houses when the war began. In this boarding house, which was luxurious by Jaffna standards, the girls shared a tiny room with not-quite polished concrete floors and white lace curtains. Through the back window of the room I stayed in I had a view of the, surprisingly, still tropical backyard. I could see that quite a large part of the back of the house was missing, the result of a mortar, the owners said, which had struck several years previously.

The girls, Vithya and Welesta, are both Tamil (not Sinhalese) and Catholic, and the house is located on the Cathedral Road, near the Cathedral that was a shelter for non-Tamils since the war began. We didn't have much time as I only met them as I was leaving. They had been too shy to come out of their room when either Siri or I was around! And in fact, the woman they called their "guardian" did not really encourage them to at all. I interviewed the girls together because they spoke a limited amount of English and Sinhalese, and as it turned out I needed each to help me translate for the other.

WE LOVE PEACE

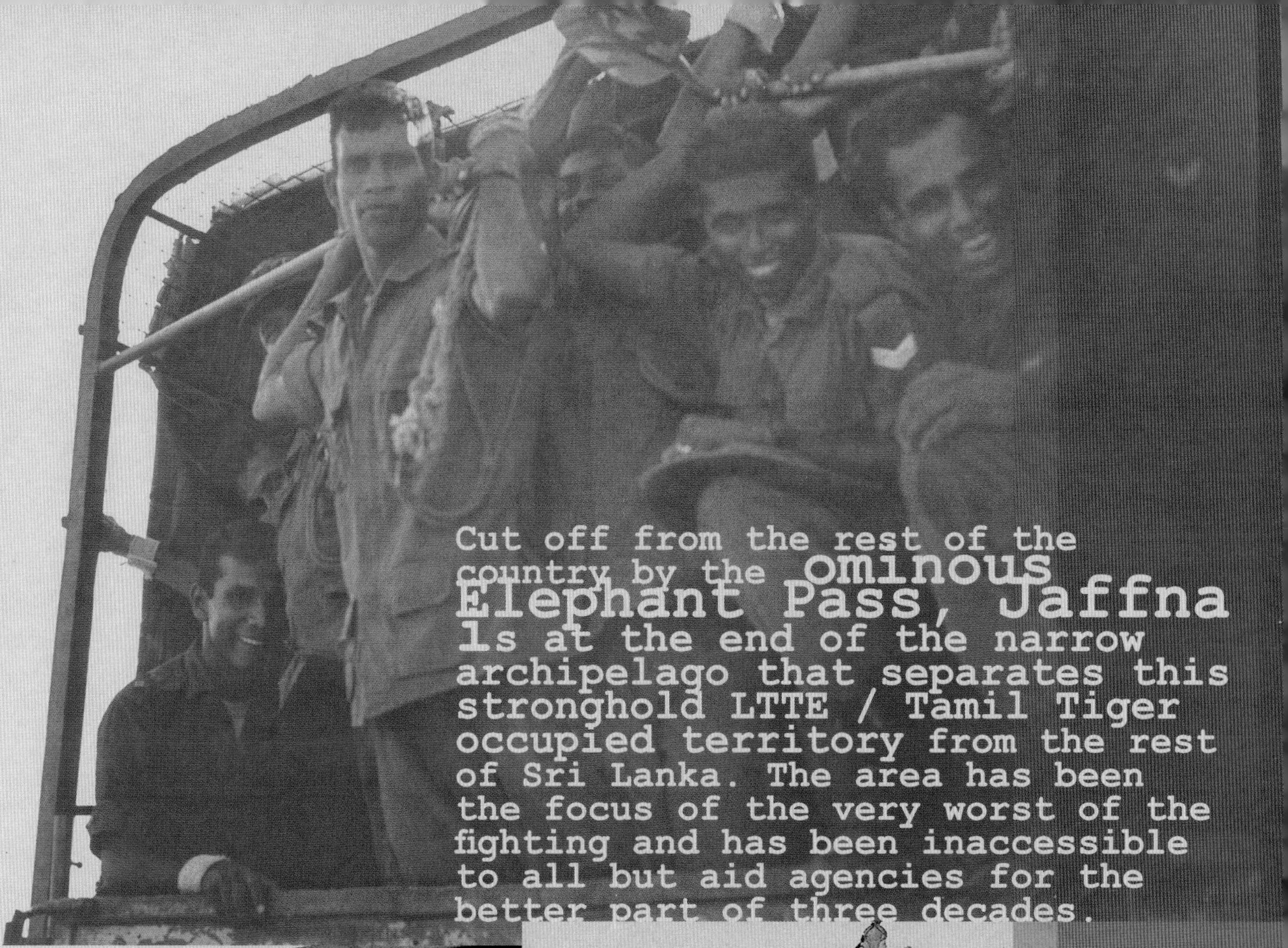

Cut off from the rest of the country by the **ominous Elephant Pass, Jaffna** is at the end of the narrow archipelago that separates this stronghold LTTE / Tamil Tiger occupied territory from the rest of Sri Lanka. The area has been the focus of the very worst of the fighting and has been inaccessible to all but aid agencies for the better part of three decades.

DANGER
BEWARE OF MINES
LANDMINES THREATEN YOUR SAFETY
LANDMINES GENERALLY INVISIBLE
THEY CANNOT TELL FRIEND FROM ENEMY
YOUR PRECAUTION ENSURES SAFETY.
IMPLEMENTED BY: unicef: WHITE PIGEON

JUDE
PRAY FOR US

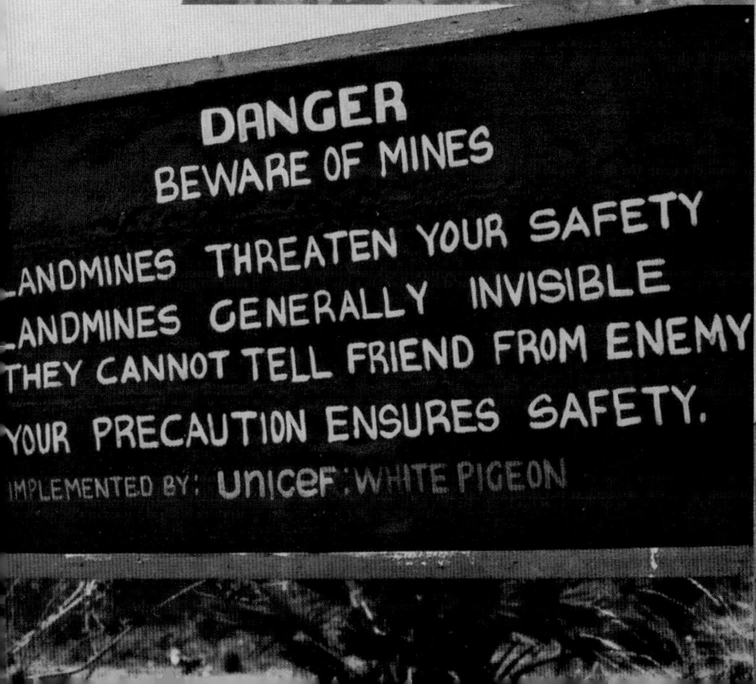

VITHYA
BERNARD REVAL:

I live with my aunty and uncle now (see postscript page 94).

I hope to finish my course, so I can become a doctor. I would like to travel and see other countries. I want to go to France and Norway for the cool climate. It gets really hot here!

We never go out at all! There was a curfew here in the town **so no one could be on the streets after dark. But since the curfew stopped [25 December 2001] we can go out if we want.** But my boyfriend lives in Mannar – he's a teacher there **– and so I don't go out much in Jaffna. I spend time doing my studies.**

In Mannar to visit my relatives I play netball on the Mannar team. But I don't do it here in Jaffna.

I do want to have a family but I have many exams to take before then!

AVE

Gnanapragasam Welesta
or "Welesta"

This is a private house where I have been living for five months. My family is from the East part of Sri Lanka, from the Mannar region and I came here to Jaffna after the ceasefire to take tuition in Bioscience at the University of Jaffna. This is for my pre-medical studies, so that I can study to be a doctor.

It's going well, my roommate, Vithya is also studying the same thing. First we have to finish one year of study, this year, and then another four years at the University of Jaffna, which has survived the war.

I don't know anyone in the LTTE [Tamil Tigers]. It [the civil war] hasn't been good for the country, people have died and the buildings have been destroyed. Too many people have been killed. Both my mother and father are dead. The LTTE killed my father at home, in Mannar. He was beaten to death.

I would like to make new friends. I want to go to Rome to see the Pope. I want to get married and have children.

We are not really allowed to go out, our guardian is very strict and my boyfriend lives in the United States, in New York so we don't see each other too much at the moment. He is a computer engineer and he is Tamil, too. I would someday like to go to New York. I like the American culture.

I visit St Mary's Church in Jaffna for praying. I believe we go to heaven when we die.

SRI LANKAN POSTSCRIPT: The civil war in Sri Lanka has seen a generation grow up missing either one or often both parents. Many adults have been killed and/or displaced as a result of a war that is as complicated as civil wars usually are. This means that tens of thousands of children have been raised and/or are spending long periods of time in orphanages or they are living in foster care with surviving relatives. Vithya, who only really spoke Tamil, was hesitant about the reasons she was living with her aunt and uncle. Tamil people are fiercely proud and dignified.

In Colombo, a Tamil man who worked with Siri gave me a (very) loose translation of a popular Tamil song, MAIYAKAMA KALAKKAMA: "Life is a beautiful cart", which basically talks about relationships, love and marriage, Tamil-style.

LIFE IS A BEAUTIFUL CART

If the two partners, the wheels on the cart
Be equal, perfect and of the same size,
There must not be even an inch of difference,
Between them.
And if you find the perfect wheel before you pull the cart,
Then you can pull the cart on any road.
In life, there are problems, you took the "rude road",
But if at that time the wheels are equal
You can still push or pull the cart.
But even if you travel on a smooth road,
If the wheels aren't equal,
You can't pull it no matter what.
Always remember that millions of others have less than you.
Always be happy and thank God for your life.
In the beginning you are going to get into trouble,
So you must change the wheel before you start the journey.

Elephant Pass, Jaffna August 2002

12
RGS

NAME: SHULYN HUNTER
D.O.B: 12.06.83
AGE: 21 YEARS OLD
NATIONALITY: AUSTRALIAN
LIVES: BROOME, WESTERN AUSTRALIA
OCCUPATION: IT CONSULTANT /
ASSISTANT

BUBBLY ALWAYS SMILING
HARD WORKER PEOPLE PERSON
AMIABLE TALKATIVE DIFFERENT
PETITE NATURAL HONEST

HER STORY:

I met Shulyn while filming on location in Broome, Western Australia. We were out on the point at Townbeach, the original port of Broome, on the far northwest coast of Australia, literally at the point where the desert meets the sea. The soil is an intense burnt sienna; the sea, two perfect shades of turquoise. The contrast is exquisite.

Shulyn had pulled up in her car and was hanging with some friends in the car park. They were watching us as we set up the next shot, under a massive baobab tree on the point. Shulyn had this field of energy surrounding her! She was so alive and energized, her aura projected all the way across the car park. Her openness and her enthusiasm were a winning combination. She was so proud of her town! And justifiably so, for Broome is famous, most notably as a pearl fishing town and as the location of the legendary Cable Beach. It is also home to the oldest outdoor picture theatre in Australia, Sun Pictures. It's that odd thing: an isolated rural town with an international airport, a Paspaley and Mikimoto pearl clad crew that somehow, amazingly, blends nonchalantly with Mom 'n Pop tourists, retirees in Winnebagos, film industry types, backpackers from practically every nation on earth and a diverse indigenous and Asian population.

Shulyn also has a gentle, sociable nature that is another reason people gravitate towards her. A local girl with an extraordinary ancestry that she carries lightly yet respectfully, Shulyn is the epitome of modern. **And cool.**

My background is Malaysian, Chinese and Aboriginal. I am the eldest of three children in my immediate family - I have two brothers and one sister. I'm from the Bardi crew [tribe]- we're the Peninsula Mob! We cover the Lombidina, Djardinjin, Cape Leveque areas, up through the Dampier Peninsula and all the way to One Arm Point. My name is Chinese and my grandfather, who raised me when I was really small, named me. He didn't even speak English, but he read the subtitles on a documentary about the Shao-lin monks and named me Shulyn after them!

Both my grandmothers are Aboriginal, but both my [biological] grandfathers were Asian. My grandfather on my mother's side was Chinese and my grandfather on my father's side was Malay. I have never met my Mum's father, but I have had three mentor-grandfather-type figures. They are not my actual family but they are very close to my family, and that is why I call them my grandfathers. One is my step-Dad's father – he's a white man and I'm very close to him. My stepfather is part-white, part-Aboriginal. He's from the Pilbara region, south of the Kimberley. One mentor-grandfather was Malay and the other of my mentor-grandfathers was from Sunday Island, close to One Arm Point. My biological father is a half-blood Aboriginal. Both my grandmothers are full-blood Aboriginal.

It's complicated for me to explain it - but it seems so natural to me and I just feel so lucky to have these people that I call my family. I've never really given it as much thought before - everybody has an interesting background I suppose!

I'm very proud of my Aboriginality and my heritage - it's unique. And I also suppose as a Broome person - being a local and being from my own town - I feel really good about it. I have a strong sense of identity. I know my town and my town's history and I know a lot of the people ... I have just finished reading a book by Diane Morissey, *The Tears of the Moon*. It's about Broome. There's so much in the book that I can relate to - in my small way!

I've even got a traditional name. My bush name is Loongi [pronounced loong-eye]. It was the name originally of one of my grandmother's grandmothers, and now it's mine too. I haven't really practiced anything truly traditional, but I guess the stories I know and having a traditional name ... it's a very unique feeling knowing they have been passed to me, that's for sure.

Talking about it gives me the sense of something that I still have to dig up. My past is ... massive! The lineage on each side has so many stories. My grandma - Nana - my Mum's mother, was one of ten children. They were all sent to a mission in Lombardina. This was in the pearling era - it was a very romantic period in Broome's history. My grandmother is a Bardi Jawi [indigenous tribe]. Somewhere between the ages of sixteen to eighteen, when she was old enough to work, she left the mission and came to Broome, which was still [racially] segregated in those days – segregation ended in about 1966. And she lived in Broome and met my Chinese grandfather when she was about twenty years old in the early 1960s. Some time after, my grandfather went away somewhere. We lost track of him after that. Then she had my mother soon after.

I'm like a butterfly, I just sort of float about and try and be nice to people and to be sweet. I'm just me.

Since I have been thinking about it, I feel as if there's kind of a part of me missing … I haven't tracked back my grandfather's story and my grandmother on my father's side either. It would be good for me to be able to put it all together. I definitely know I need to address all the footsteps that came before mine. I especially want to know my grandfather's family history, so I can tell my children where they came from too.

My family is really amazing even though I'm not necessarily related to them all by blood. I still regard them as my family. Blood is not the only tie. It's more about true acceptance and understanding. Each person in my family has their own beliefs and values but we are so tight. **We are the tightest crew you could ever come across!**

I work at the markets and, when it's a full moon, the moon reflects on the mud flats at low tide. I sell donuts for my [other] grandfather, 'cos he has a little caravan food stall. I just help out my family – it's what we all do for each other. **I really like the diversity and the beliefs that my family has. It has allowed me to approach life in an open, accepting way. I am amiable and willing to learn things. I'm open to life I think. Everything to me is so – WOW!**

I sometimes think that people take advantage of belonging to a certain culture, and I don't agree with that. But really I'm just proud to be me. I made the top-twelve Aboriginal girls' calendar in 2000. Nothing really happened for me as a result, even though I was told it would be really good for some sort of career … but I'm happy with whatever comes. Just because I'm Aboriginal, doesn't mean that I should get any special treatment, I feel special enough. If you want to be accepted in the general mainstream of the population, you don't need to shout about it. Don't cry unique – BE unique! I'm proud to be who I am and where I'm from. That's enough for me. Just as long as I give a share of what I have, to each and every person that I come across in life, and as long as they are happy with what I have to give, I'm happy. Everybody has their own set of beliefs and values. I just try to keep it as simple as that.

I work part-time at a telecenter (that's my main job) and I'm studying IT [information technology]. I'm pretty much a clerical assistant, assisting people with technical problems. I also work for the Kimberley Development Commission. It's a government job and it's pretty clerical, but I learn a lot about the whole region.

When you look at the new generation in our region, it is not so much about the pearling era any more. Things have changed in the town and the population and the genetics of the new generation reflect that. All my friends have dark skin and they all have some kind of Asian heritage as well. I think I have the typical Broome look because I am the product of the genetic pool of the pearling era. I always think my friends and I all look the same! The kids today look more individual, a little bit more Causcasian and a bit less Asiatic. The people mix in Broome has changed because the town has really opened up in the past few decades.

I would love to go to the Greek Islands. I have studied a bit of Greek mythology and language while I was in primary school. **I have a fascination with the Greek culture. My Greek teacher said I have the tongue for it!** I would like to go to Paris and travel around Europe. I would eventually like to get out of Broome for at least a part of my life. Otherwise, you could get stuck in just a local mentality, and there's a very big world out there.

[illegible] re's a purpose for my life. I believe in karma, [illegible] re. You should always be true to yourself 'cos if you don't, you'll have to live up to it later! Sometimes it is hard to be true to yourself because you may not know what you want at the time. Life is mysterious, you don't know what the future holds. Things change and not many people pick up on the opportunities that happen. If you miss out or you ignore them as they present themselves, it's like missing a bus. Some people have opportunities that roll up at the door and that's probably because they did something good before that.

Karma comes both good and bad. That is something my Nana tells me. She has little names for things and reads the signs. Nana is spiritual - she claims she is![laughs] Even though she grew up in the missions, it could never be extinguished, it's so natural for her. Nana lives a very mysterious and a bit of a secretive life. She writes all the time. She's always writing lots of things about her upbringing and her life. There is a lot of energy around her, I reckon there is a lot in the future for her to tell us yet, things we don't know about our past. But I'm still pretty young, so there's time to find out!

[illegible] spin myself out because I mention [illegible] and then it will happen. Intuition has [illegible] a dose of your future somehow. It gives [illegible] signs leading up to it. Nana is the same [illegible] a sense of something about to happen. She's [illegible], "I am going to see someone today …"

I went through a lot of healing during the ages of seventeen to twenty because I had gone through a bad stage after a relationship. I was sad all the time. I was depressed. It was over family matters really. Your family is your circle, and because of a relationship I felt, detached from my circle. I couldn't get myself out of the depressed state I was in and this could have detached my spirit from the body. It was like I had an out-of-body experience.

To heal myself I went to crystal healing, aromatherapy, acupuncture, I worked on opening up my chakras. I was singing to deal with the emotions. That would bring me to tears and I had a lot of overwhelming feelings. I got into tarot cards, books, everything![laughs] I went to a crystal healer who said she felt the presence of an older woman, one of my ancestors, near a tree - an indigenous woman. I felt it was my grandmother and that she was healing me through the crystal healer. I felt really spun out. Afterwards I asked my Nana, "Were you with me today?" She will never tell me the real answer! But things got better so something shifted! In my way I am similar. And I believe in knowing when you meet someone that they are meant for you. You've got to have a soulmate! I reckon maybe my big one's on the way![laughs]

[illegible] pportive mother and open to ideas. Even if she doesn't like an idea [illegible] s me a deeper insight into what I've thought of so that I can make [illegible] n. My Mum is pretty cool like that - and we can both think things through in depth. She knows that if she says no, I'll just rebel straightaway! She knows me well - she's like my best friend. I'm pretty close with my two younger siblings.

When I went to Bali in Indonesia, everyone kept asking me if I was Indonesian: "Are you from the south island?" Bali was a spinout because we never sort of realized what we have here at home. You tend to appreciate what you have more when you miss something. Another thing about Bali that really struck me was the dancing.

The music from the gamelan [classic Balinese instrument] is pretty full-on, and their eyes all wide – it is incredible. A different culture is so exciting to me. It was spun out! But it was like a connection for me too. You get such a strong connection with a culture when song and dance comes into it.

When we celebrate Shinju Matsuri Festival, which happens in Broome every year around the September full moon, I feel a connection with all my cultures! Shinju Matsuri is the Festival of the Pearl. One year I did Malay dancing with handkerchiefs and empty coconut shells. I learned how to do it from an older Malay man. It didn't take me long to learn how to use my wrists and move around in a circle with the other girls who were dancing. I loved doing that sort of dancing.

When we were in Bali, my Aboriginal grandfather passed away in the middle of the trip. **My Mum felt it and she got really sick in the middle of the trip. My aunt got in touch with us to tell us. Your "leeun" is your spirit or your gut feeling, your intuition or your sixth sense.** It tells you things. My Mum's leeun was trying to communicate about my grandfather. She didn't know exactly what it was at the time, but when my aunty called with the bad news, it made sense. Mum went and saw him specially before we left for Bali. We buried him not far from his tree – his dreaming was in a particular tree in One Arm Point. A charter plane flew him around the islands – his dead body I mean – and this was how they brought his spirit home. They brought him home to One Arm Point. The tree of his dreaming overlooks the Indian Ocean. We all went to his funeral, which was held at the traditional burial site for the people from the Bardi tribe at Gumanun, in between Cape Leveque and One Arm Point.

I'd like to go to Kuala Lumpur in Malaysia. That's another part of my heritage, but I've never really looked into it. I'd like to go and see the more natural sights there – the wildlife would be interesting and so would the spa thing! I'd like to get buried in the mud and do the spa thing.[laughs]

My white grandfather used to take me to Sunday School because he was trying to bring me up Christian. I was a little baldheaded thing! I used to run through the shopping center and sing out "Praise the Lord". I'd be singing out "Hallelujah" in the middle of the mall. I was this little black kid running around with a bald head and long socks and praising the Lord! Mum reckons my grandfather used to duck he was so embarassed. [laughs] I don't follow any religion now. I just refer to my leeun – my spirit. **My intuition is pretty much my God. I love God and I believe in God but I regard it as being within me.**

The most unusual and amazing thing about me would be that even though I'm a single unit, I'm not single really – I have so many people around me! I don't know what I'd do without them. My family unit is pretty much what has kept me together.

Best memory of my life
I have so many
Everything I ca
recall is so great
But maybe what I want in life coul
be on the verge of happening an
SO MY BEST MEMORY IS
YET TO COME

13
RGS

NAME: DALIA 'DJ GROOVY D' PROGLI
D.O.B: 10.09.75
AGE: 29 YEARS OLD
NATIONALITY: AUSTRALIAN
LIVES: SYDNEY
OCCUPATION: DJ / MUSIC PRODUCER

HER STORY:

I met Dalia at the departure lounge of Sydney's Kingsford Smith Airport. DJ "Groovy D", as she is known in the club scene, was on her way to the United States to meet up with her old friend and college roommate, Bree. Wheeling her record case into the lounge, and with her hoop earrings swinging, Dalia looked crisp and alert under a truckie's cap. A plane flight is always a thing of anticipation for most people, but this is especially so for Dalia. For a girl who almost never relaxes, she was - even though she didn't look it - tired and mostly excited to catch up on sleep!

A DJ's work is never done – well, at least not til the wee hours. And as one of Sydney's busiest Hip Hop DJs, Dalia's always got a lot on her plate. With a radio show to produce and long hours of studio time to log for her own music as well as doing gigs, Dalia juggles her 'worklifestyle' with Cirque du Soleil flair. With her tremendous work ethic and a strong vision of her direction in life she is a girl who is clearly on a mission. Confident in herself and of her skills, she's a night owl with a passion for beats and mixing it up. Ever cool, Dalia takes it on.

My body is my temple,
and I trust my gut instinct.
THAT'S PRETTY MUCH MY
RELIGION.

My parents are Hungarian. My Mum and Dad were born in Hungary and my brother, who is ten years older than me, was born in Transylvania [Romania]. My mother's family moved to Israel due to the communist occupation of Hungary. Then my parents moved to Israel and I was born in Bersheba, near Jerusalem. We came to Australia in 1977 when I was two. I speak, read and write Hungarian but I haven't been back to Israel since I was nine unfortunately. I can remember soldiers carrying machineguns in the streets. The situation there is just so hard core with the war. I really wish I could visit my relatives because I have hundreds of relatives there. I can visit the ones in Hungary but it's a much smaller family. Whereas in Israel it's HUGE. I can't wait to go back. I identify strongly with Europe and the Middle East, because of my background.

My parents are Catholic, and although I was born in Israel, I'm not Jewish, I don't have a religion as such. **I just believe in the Universe and I look after myself.**

My parents are fantastic, they came from a poor situation and never had much of an education, so they just wanted to give me everything they never had. I was so busy with piano lessons, ballet, tap dancing, physical culture, Hungarian dance and scouts. Every day there was something. I went to a Catholic school five days of the week and a Hungarian school on the sixth day. My Mum and Dad gave me my work ethic and my sense of responsibility and they worked so hard to give me opportunities.

In 1994/95 I was studying art theory and psychology at Miami University in Florida in the United States. That's where I met my close friend Bree. How we met was serendipity. My first roommate at the university was an Italian opera singer who used half a can of hairspray on her hair every day and there were no windows in our room, so I had to move out! And then I moved in with Bree as her roommate, which has turned into a lifelong friendship. She's my "bestest" friend because she's just so easygoing and I love being around her. There's no one like her. Maybe the distance helps, so we don't get sick of each other! We write to each other at least once a week and we've kept that going for seven years. I think that's pretty rare. Typically I write really long letters and she gives me one line replies, so that's pretty funny. But that's just Bree. I'm in my element when I'm happily playing music and hanging with my best friend. After seven years, nothing has changed between us, even though we live in different countries. I think it just shows that once there's a connection it is forever, but I've never had that with anyone before.

I have been a DJ in Sydney for seven years, since I was twenty-one years old. I was always interested in the skating and underground music scenes. I started doing it as an extra job really. **It was a hobby to start off with but with the amount of money I've invested in it... I no longer call it just a hobby!** It's crazy how much debt I've put myself in – to the tune of thousands and thousands of dollars. I don't mind because even though records are so expensive, I buy them for my radio show as well. I'm going to continue spending on records – I have to. That's just how it is!

I'm the only girl DJ who has a radio show in Sydney, who does production and who specializes in Hip Hop. The amount of female Hip Hop DJs in Sydney who get gigs – well I can count them on one hand. Before the rise of the MC, DJs kept the party going and the MC was just there to hype the crowd. Then all of a sudden a whole lot of money got behind Hip Hop, so MCs were getting all the record deals and the DJ was just pushed to the back – hence the "Return of The DJ" as a concept! I've done a mixed CD with re-mixes and a few with vocals as well as four live mixes that I made as well as an original track. I pressed that to a white label and that's what I gave out as a promotion thing. That set me back about [Australian]$300, for twenty-five copies, just to get it mastered in Detroit. It was all done through a record label … I'm pretty excited just to have my own stuff on record! One of my dreams is to meet [the Hip Hop impresario] Russell Simmons.

I just want to present myself more professionally. Guys are the ones who book DJs mostly, so sometimes it's hard when I get passed over for one of their mates for a DJ booking, but a few of the guys have been more supportive and booked me. It will help me to assert myself and to present myself even more professionally to get the gigs I believe I deserve to get. Not just as a gender-based thing either. I have mastered my skills and I have so much fun playing music for other people. I wanna make more beats and produce more tracks … I get really frustrated not being able to find enough music that is made by women!

I don't like the general representation of WOMEN IN HIP HOP – but I don't want to give my energy to thinking about it though, because it's too negative. I just want to focus on doing my own thing. I don't like to give my power away! Australian women seem to be very strong and very much in their own element and very much in control – in the Hip hop scene at least. They are definitely misunderstood because the guys don't know how to take them. They are still learning how to deal with strong women who really know what they want and are going for it. The guys can get intimidated and they don't like being second best – or not being the main focus.

From living in Miami, I came to the conclusion that female-male relations are culturally influenced. The underground scene in anything is way cooler than the mainstream for both genders. There are a lot of grassroots artists in the underground scene, which shows that it is thriving and it isn't based on traditional roles or expectations. The mainstream generalisations are the female sexual stereotypes – it's just like guys with the guns and violence thing. Those damaging elements are always going to be there, just like pornography – it's never going away.

I would never put myself on display for a guy's pleasure. There are other ways to make money. My way of dealing with situations like that is to focus my energy elsewhere. I would rather focus my energy on positive things and outlets, but it really does make me quite angry seeing pornography being available from newspaper boxes. Any kid could go along and buy that. The porn depicts such stereotypes too – it's all Asian girls and college girls! Those men must be really uncreative and stupid to be into that kind of stuff. But a lot of people – guys – learn about sex from porn. And that's not very healthy because they start off by learning that women are there just to pleasure them.

NEVADA
WASSUP

I feel like I know who I am and have done so for a long while, but I get frustrated other people don't understand me and just start judging me. My close girlfriends know me and respect me though and I respect them back. You need time to form bonds with people and for them to get to know you properly. Trying to spend time with friends and family with the amount of time I spend doing what I do is very hard. It can test a friendship or a relationship and that's why I do my best be organized, so I can spend quality time with people I love. But it's hard when I have commitments that conflict with social things I'd prefer to do.

It's hard to have time for a boyfriend, and I'm actually single at the moment. I've been out of a long-term relationship since early 2003, which has been a relief actually. It was a self-destructive relationship and now it's healthier and probably better 'cos we're separated by a lot of distance. I think love can be very blind sometimes. I'm one of those people that only hook up when it's something meaningful. But maybe I really need to break out of that! It's just taking me a long time to get over things and be free enough to even want to go there. **I'm a thinker and my brain governs everything.**

But I have a cat! Her name is Chi, which means "life force" and "the flow of energy". She just flows in and flows out. She's the real love of my life.[laughs]

My world revolves around being in the studio, at the radio station, at gigs or at home. So it's hard to meet people strangely enough. **I would love to find someone who I could be really content with and be really happy with.** Someone who would support me as much as I would support them. I really don't know when that's going to happen. Plus I have to finish doing what I want to do first.

I have a no-exercise policy! [laughs] It's more important to sleep. DJs sleep a lot. Usually if I've got a gig – I work full-time – I get about three hours a night. Depends on what other missions I've got to do! I just run on empty sometimes, that's why I get colds a lot. I've been doing it for a while now, 'cos I work full-time and I do my radio show and on weekends I do gigs as well. I need my holidays for rest and recovery. Being able to sleep is wonderful. Sleep is a great concept. My plans whenever I don't have anything on are to sleep. I carry my records and I run across the road to gigs, and I dance a bit while I'm on my feet working … that's enough exercise!

If I had them, I would like my kids to be proactive and follow their dreams. I'd probably ask them what they'd like to do as opposed to telling them what chores they had to do. My parents were pretty strict when I was younger and I wasn't allowed to have a boyfriend or watch certain movies. So my kids would probably have it a bit easier … [laughs]

When I went to the States I pierced my tongue and I got a septum ring and tattooes, and I would go out and was much more independent generally. So when I came back they kind of freaked out because I was pretty wild for a bit and I started expressing myself a lot more. But they're pretty cool now - they're both softies really! I think they are proud of me now, and they see how committed I am to my work and my music. I have so much respect for them because they have done so much for me and given me everything they could.

Sundays have never been good days for me. It was the one day of the week when everyone was home and it was pretty full-on when there was tension in the house. I used to hang out the front a lot by myself. My parents divorced in 2003. They have both found love again - which is pretty amazing as they're not young - and I'm just happy for them. My Mum's getting married in Hawaii soon!

My lifelong dream would be to find a cap that fits my head! I have a really tiny head and caps don't fit. I try them on everywhere I go … It's a DJ thing! [laughs] Actually, my ultimate dream is to do commercial radio - a Hip Hop show that was commercially viable. I love presenting music on radio. And I'd also love to do an all-female Hip Hop album that includes voices from all over Australia. I'd love to go to the Northern Territory and record Aboriginal voices and record beats and tracks with them. I want to mix street free styling and various genres of music with Hip Hop, and come up with some nice experimental tracks. Studio time and equipment is so expensive!

ULTIMATELY I JUST WANT THE FREEDOM TO DO WHATEVER I WANT CREATIVELY.

NAME: LINDSAY GREEN
D.O.B: 16.09.81
AGE: 23 YEARS OLD
NATIONALITY: AUSTRALIAN
LIVES: BRISBANE,
QUEENSLAND, AUSTRALIA
OCCUPATION: TEACHER

14
RGS

HER STORY:
Lindsay contacted me a couple of years ago and asked me if she could be involved in any new or future girlosophy projects. I was on an extended stay in Bali, Indonesia, wrapping up *The Breakup Survival Kit*, however we stayed in touch. We missed each other on several occasions when I was in Brisbane or the Gold Coast, and she was teaching in Townsville, having moved to Far North Queensland to take up a full-time teaching position. When we eventually met, it was like meeting up with a long-lost friend.

Though her navigation skills are questionable - based as they are on the serendipity of being Lindsay more than on driving prowess - Lindsay is one of the smartest, kindest, compassionate people you could meet! She is extremely tolerant, brooks no rubbish on anything that is discriminatory and she is passionately interested in the arts. She is open to all aspects of humanity. These qualities would make her a fabulous teacher, with the kind of influence students would surely look back upon in later life and think, "Miss Green was cool!" Each person should be so lucky to have a Miss Green in the early years! For Lindsay navigates her life with poise and confidence. And we can all benefit from a teacher like her at just about any time.

DYNAMIC LOYAL SENSITIVE
SUBTLE DETERMINED GENUINE
NEUROTIC! SILLY AESTHETE
DRAMATIC

I grew up in Aspley, a suburb of Brisbane, in Queensland. **I had a very happy childhood with lots of family around me.** I have two brothers, one older and one younger than me – and we are so different from each other, which always makes life interesting!

I am a qualified teacher and early in 2004 I moved to Townsville in Far North Queensland to teach drama and English at a high school. These subjects are fantastic for exploring social issues. I definitely operate from a socially critical basis! I have written and taught units of work on such issues as mental illness, racism and the Australian identity.

I was a conscientious child! I was well behaved, high achieving, creative and studious, but I never really felt like I had a place. I had heaps of friends but I didn't feel I was in my "niche". I always felt I was missing something! [laughs] I also tend to worry about things all the time. I loved reading, and I was quite a solitary child. I used to walk around reading and bump into things. I remember Mum used to invite other kids around to play with me, but I used to get cranky and want them to go home!

But then one day I auditioned for a play and things changed. I had done drama since early in school. The play was not connected with school, it was through the community theater. There were about one hundred people at the audition, but they only needed to cast ten people.

I had a fun day and I wanted the role so badly! Then I got the call-back and I won a part in the play. It was a defining moment because for the first time in my life I met people outside of my normal world. They showed me a potential way of life that I had only envisaged. I didn't actually know if it existed!

ALL I KNEW WAS WHITE MIDDLE CLASS. I'D NEVER MET ANYONE WHO WAS HOMOSEXUAL, OR IN THEIR TWENTIES, OR LEADING AN ART-BASED CREATIVE LIFE. THEY SEEMED TO BE MORE LIKE THE WAY I FELT I WAS. AND WHAT I WANTED TO BE.

When I was fourteen years old, my father committed suicide after suffering from clinical depression for many years. One day, I came home and Mum told us, "Dad's in hospital, he is ve stressed at work and he is not very well". To me, at the time, it seemed like he was just hav a rest. We didn't understand what was really happening – we were given simple explanations. W used to visit him and take him to the park and play cricket.

Adolescence is a pretty crucial period in anyone's life. To lose a par was devastating for all of us. The sudden tragedy caused my adolescence to be a particularly turbulent time. I had not been aware of his illness until two weeks before his death and I struggled to understand what had happened and why. We were all grief stricken. Apparently my father had suffered from clinical depression since he was twenty-five years old. I worried tha mother would die and my brothers and I would be left alone. My parents had been together all my life.

I believe suicide is so horrendous. It is the person you love who has knowingly caused the p and chosen to end their own life. I feel so sad when I think of the pain my father must have felt, to have made that decision.

I AM STARTING TO UNDERSTAND AN ACCEPT THIS TRAGEDY AND FEEL EXTREMELY POSITIVE ABOUT MY LIFE AND THE POSSIBILITIES.

I've started talking to Mum about it, now that I am older able to understand it more. There are such misconceptions about depression. I know quite a few people who are on an depressants. And yet I have also heard things like "Why w so-and-so be depressed? She's gorgeous". But it has nothi to do with appearances or personality! It's to do with th chemical makeup of a person.

Prior to taking up my full-time teaching position, I had to teach a book, *Lockie Leonard,* by Tim Winton. It's a pretty full-on book about a boy's mother who goes into hospital with depression. Obviously it was quite close to home and at first I thought about saying no, bu

This Emile Zola quote is my favorite: "If you asked me what I came into this world to do, **I will tell you.**

I CAME TO LIVE OUT LOUD."

AND OF COURSE EVERYONE IS WORRIED ABOUT YOUNG WOMEN AND THE OBSESSION WITH APPEARANCES.

WOMEN FEEL LESS BEAUTIFUL IF THEY'RE NOT DRESSED WELL,

whereas men don't identify so closely with the clothes they wear. I think it is because women are more looked at in general. Men look at women and women look at women!

I thought, "Who better to teach it?" My Mum is a physiotherapist and she helped me to arrange a guest speaker to come in from a mental health unit at a hospital. It turned out to be an amazing experience and the guest speaker spoke to all the kids about what mental illness is. I learned so much too! We were talking about misconceptions. Mental illness can be triggered by many factors. Extreme stress, poor diet, a lack of exercise, or even taking mind-altering substances such as ecstasy and marijuana are all triggers. Taking these substances even once can increase a person's chances of developing a mental illness. In my case, my father was a doctor - he was a general practitioner - so the extreme stress made sense to me.

I didn't actually tell the children that I had personal experiences that were similar to the book. At the time to tell the story to thirty teenagers was too difficult. Even though it would have added another dimension, at the time **I wasn't ready to be that naked in front of them.** But I felt like I'd done something that was worthwhile. I changed their perception of what a mental illness is forever. You hear loose use of words all the time in schools. I gave them something to think about after school! In the end, they had a much wider understanding about mental illness.

I went to Queensland University of Technology and I graduated in 2003. When I started studying at university I wanted to do acting. **I acted in lots of plays and put on plays as well, I felt like I could do more using my drama in a socially beneficial and community-conscious way. I didn't want it to be all about me! And as an actor it can be a bit of a self-hating profession with so much emphasis on what you look like.** The way I see it, the purpose of acting is not necessarily to become someone like Mel Gibson. Lots of acting students and their parents think that's what acting is for, to become an actor and therefore someone famous. There's so much more to it than that!

The point of acting for me is to explore social issues in a new way and for educational purposes. I also like it because the kids are always excited to come to drama lessons and therefore they tend to like the drama teacher! I see all the kids that are ostracized and I try to make all kids understand about tolerance. Children use the words "poofter", "faggot", "gay" as everyday slang insults. They have the narrowest preconceptions and I pick them up on it all the time. **I want to use my position as a teacher to widen students' perceptions of what they can be.**

I'm also really interested in gender construction in society - the way being masculine or feminine is presented. Every facet constructs the "right way" to be female or the "right way" to be male. This goes through everything from subject choices in school, magazines and stereotyping, sports that are chosen and even toy catalogues. **HOW COME BARBIE'S FEET DON'T FIT INTO ANYTHING BUT HIGH HEELS?!**

I didn't stay at my job in Townsville, I ended up being there for about six weeks and it wasn't right. It was quite full-on having to resign, but I have realized that I need to be around my friends and family and that even the best job isn't worth it if you're away from those you love. My friends and family have such a calming influence on me and when I was away I felt like I had no anchor and the stress was too much. So now I'm home again and I'm taking on part-time teaching work until a full-time position that I would like becomes available. **Things always work out for the best!**

powerful
fun in love
excitable
passionate
proud
inquisitive
committed
disciplined

NAME: CRYSTAL SIMPSON
D.O.B: 17.06.85
AGE: 19 YEARS OLD
NATIONALITY: AUSTRALIAN
LIVES: YALLINGUP, WESTERN AUSTRALIA
OCCUPATION: SURF SHOP OWNER / SURFER

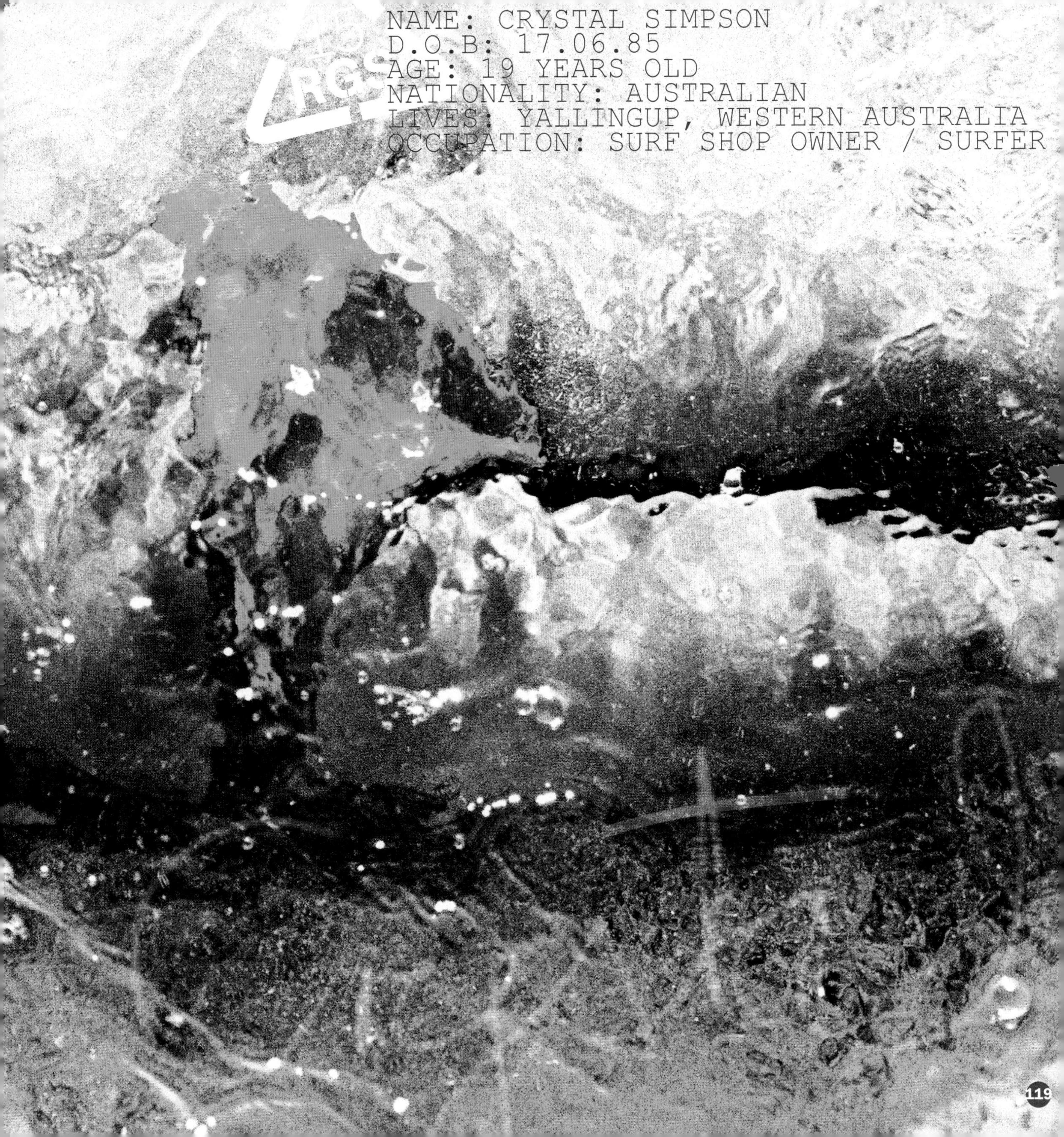

I've always been close to nature – it feels wrong to live in the city

HER STORY:

I first met Crystal and her family – the [other!] extraordinary Simpsons – when I went to the Margaret River region in the southwest of Western Australia to produce material for girlosophy – *The Love Survival Kit*. Crystal is one of the girlosophy-sponsored surfers, and her outlook on life is a brilliant mix of positivity and courageousness. Over the past few years I have watched Crystal transform from a shy and reserved girl into the confident, expressive person she is today. Although she left school early, at fifteen, now at just eighteen years of age, she owns and manages a surf shop that she has turned into a thriving business. Whether attending leadership courses or regularly participating in surfing contests, Crystal tackles the **challenges in her life** with both a **cool grace** and an uncommon **clarity**.

my family is Outrageous! I grew up on a fishing boat

that my parents bought when they started their fishing business in the early eighties. It was a commercial fishing boat of about seventy feet [twenty-one meters] in length and we lived on the boat for several years. My parents got together when they were quite young. My Mum had been traveling in India and she was about seventeen. She met my father when she just got back. Although my Dad was originally from Cottesloe in Perth, he moved down to Yallingup [on the southwest coast of Western Australia]. Together they moved up north to Point Samson, in the Pilbara region [on the north west cape of Australia where the Indian Ocean meets the desert] after they were married. By the time I was born they had built a cottage. I have an older brother and two younger sisters.

I don't recall ever being lonely!

My older brother, Jason, was actually born on the boat, which was called "The Westerly", and we grew up mucking around in fishing nets and playing on the coral reefs in the Kimberley region at a place called Nichol Bay. We pretty much spent our babyhood nude on the deck in the sun! The Kimberley is a really isolated and unpopulated part of the country, more of an indigenous area known for its fishing, pearls and its incredible Aboriginal history. We go camping up north for the winter every year to a surf camp in the Pilbara region, [another vast piece of desert country south of the Kimberley, known for its fishing and iron ore deposits]. **I love the desert and the ocean up there.**

There is a relatedness with everything when you experience the extremes.

I live in the southwest region of Western Australia, in Yallingup, near Margaret River, three hours drive south of the capital, Perth. I rent an apartment that I share with my younger sister. It's right next door to my family though, so I get to see them all the time, which is great.

We used to go to school down south in the summer and go to a different school in the north in winter. These days we make a surf camp at the beginning of the winter season. We go to the far north coast, right on the Indian Ocean - as it is said up there - "where the desert meets the sea". It's great fun once everyone arrives and it attracts a lot of big wave surfers from all over the world. A lot of them do tow-in surfing there - these days we all drive jetskis. Getting worked by the reef is a bit scary though, I always cut my feet and so **I'm forever doing my own first aid!**

All the bad stuff used to happen to me! I remember Jason and I would collect baitfish from the lagoon and sell them in the caravan park [a mobile home park or local trailer park] after school. One day, I think I was about eight years old, I stepped in an octopus hole and the octopus wrapped itself all around my leg. I screamed so loud that my mother could hear me all the way from a house on the hill. Poor Mum, she freaked out I think - because the reef had blue ringed octopus, stonefish - some of the most dangerous marine life in the world. Jason was just laughing so hard that he was almost unable to get it off me!

I'm really close to Jason, we've got twin energy. I'm probably a little bit more mature! [laughs] We do the same things and have the same friends, and there's that energy where **we don't have to justify our relationship, we can just let it be.** It's been good to have an older brother. They look out for you, even though they never say they do. He's so protective and I have learned so much from him. Especially when I went through that puberty age when drugs and alcohol came in. But he never wants me or my sisters to go hard or do anything that would damage ourselves, so he's very caring. He's just beautiful to me - he bought me a gold necklace with a dolphin on it - and he has a raw beauty about him that I admire. He's good, he just deals with whatever's going on in his own way.

My parents ROCK!

Mum and Dad are such pioneers. Mum is part Noongar [indigenous tribe from Western Australia] and she has a spirit to her that's rare. My Dad is such an adventurer. He has this crazy energy! I think we have had an amazing opportunity in life because even when we didn't have much money, we always had a good house and car – we had what we needed. It's a life of extremes where we come from – from down south where we live to up north on the fishing boats – it's such a huge contrast. Between the two areas you get extremes of weather, environment and people. In this part of the world you've got Aboriginal communities, rough red necks, cool surfies and a café-culture city life. And all this against a crazy landscape and the wildest weather! There is a relatedness with everything when you experience the extremes.

I don't feel any more or any less about knowing my Aboriginal background. It's just who I am. I've always been close to nature – it feels wrong to live in the city – so there's a definite link there, but it's not an overly huge part of my life. **I don't see any difference between Noongar and not. We're all human.**

The shop was an established one at my local surfing break. When it came up for sale my parents asked me if I would like to run the shop, to take it on as my full responsibility. I thought it would be unreal and I really wanted to do it. And so they bought the business for me. First of all I changed the name to "Surfside Beach Shack" and while it was already stocked when we bought the business, I have since changed all the stock in the past couple of years and renovated the interior of the shop. So it's a completely different business because, aside from two existing stocklines, I have replaced everything else with new brands. I guess you could say it used to be more "touristy", but I have made the emphasis, the beach and coastal lifestyle here. I place orders for stock through agents all over Australia. And I have learned so much from the whole experience, because running your own business is full-on, to say the least! You have to indent order nearly a whole year in advance so you're always guessing what people are going to want to buy in a year's time. But I really enjoy it because I love surfing so this is an extension of that really.

Right now, from what I've learned **I feel like I can kind of tackle anything. I'm like: bring it on!**

I left school early, in year 11, just before my sixteenth birthday. I didn't see school was going to provide me with an answer to what I wanted to do with my life – and I didn't want to waste time! My parents were really supportive of my decision and that's one of the reasons why we decided to get the surf shop. I have been doing some self-development and leadership courses that help me to achieve my goals with my business and with my surfing. I attend lectures and seminars in Perth, Sydney and Melbourne at various conference centers. I want to get my business to certain levels and I want to attain higher levels of technical excellence in my surfing as well, and the courses give me the structure to address both of these areas in my life. And I may study formally again later … I'll just see what happens.

I hope to win at the National Longboarding Championships at Bells Beach in Victoria [another state in Australia] in October 2005. Before that though, I have to get through the State Championships of Western Australia in March 2005. I feel confident that I've got what it takes to reach those levels. I'm not ranked yet, but I will be next year! [laughs] I'd love to be a professional surfer eventually, but I have so much fun anyway.

I felt like an outsider for the longest time.

The scariest thing I've ever had happen in the ocean was in a surfing contest at Yallingup on the southwest coast of Western Australia - it's a well-known big-wave surfing spot right where I live and the waves were eight to ten foot. The wave sets were coming fast, which makes it scary and hard physically because you have to paddle so much more. I got caught inside the rock reef and I took a lot of waves on the head. I didn't think I was going to get enough air at one point because I kept getting pushed down. But I made it in to the shore and now I feel stoked because they were the wildest conditions I've ever been out in.

It's empowering to state where you're going to be 'cos then it's something that you're going to "live into". And it's great to tell other people what you aim to do, so they support you to do the same. It's about working out where you're going too. So, after doing the leadership course, I've set a goal that I'm going to tell two people a day that I'm going to be the Longboarding State Champion. And then they'll start seeing me as that. **I start by saying: "That's what I'm gonna be, that's what I'm gonna do."**

When you do that they think, "Whoa, this girl means business". And then if everyone sees me as the absolute surfer girl of the world [laughs] then it's easier for me to live up to it. They believe it and then so do I. **Sharing where you want to be can be absolutely empowering.**

Having a team is the best way to get where you're going. They'll say, "Yes, you CAN" when you think, "No, I can't". They keep you there. The team is my mentor group and the encouragement I receive is the key. And I'm trying to keep it fun, as if I'm playing a game, so I don't get too attached to the outcome. It won't be as powerful if I have an attachment to the result. I have to keep any goal as a fun thing, rather than a "do-or-die thing" or a boring chore.

All the guys I knew were my friends and you wouldn't go there! It felt like they never looked at me in a sexual way. It was the "Ah, you're my sister" kind of thing. So I just went to myself, "God, get a hobby!" I took up surfing and it all started to change after that. I see a lot of young girls today and think they should get into some sort of activity, they need something to take their minds off looking good and getting a boyfriend. Girls are way too hung up on that stuff. The ones who are more laid-back have more hobbies and they're not so focused on the physical. They are too busy doing stuff they enjoy! They get ahead more in life anyhow, because they're not trying too hard. And so when they come to get a job or to study, there's room for it already - it's not going to interrupt them "looking good".

I see three major problems facing young women: the issue of having sex at such a young age, the access everyone has these days to serious drugs, and the acceptance of themselves at every age and stage. Sex is happening at too young an age for most. I mean the legal age is sixteen and the average of those who are sexually active is thirteen. Girls give blow jobs to be accepted by guys, but boys have more respect when you don't do it! And I hate it when girls tease guys in a sexual way - it's so wrong - and a lot of the time girls can't meet the expectation that they put out anyway. Using sex to get what you want and knowing you're doing it - I don't think it's right. But I think it happens a lot.

Drugs are so bad and there are so many out there! People now are even abusing attention deficit disorder drugs – all sorts of stuff that make it possible for kids to stay up all night and party. I mean it's hard to say, because it's so much a part of the growing up / youth experience but a lot of kids don't get that you can die from excessive drinking or drugtaking.

It's too readily available if anyone wants to try it. The main thing is that if you want to do it, you have to have people around you who can look after you and, if necessary, support you through the process. You can't completely control yourself on drugs and it's not worth the next day's regrets.

Yeah – there are a lot of decisions I go, "Fuck I wish I could change that!" But everything is happening and happens for a reason. I know this because when I was fifteen, a few of my friends were losing their virginity and getting boyfriends. I didn't know why it wasn't happening for me. I kept thinking "What's wrong with me?" but I knew I didn't want to have sex. Instead I began to think, "Am I fat, ugly, am I this … am I that?" It was doing my head in. This went on for a few years. I was so wrapped up in not having a boyfriend! I felt so terrible when my close friends were doing what seemed to be really adult things. It all changed when I met my current boyfriend, and I'm so proud of myself that I waited for the right person, but it happened so much later for me than for anyone else I knew. But it's not worth worrying about it all when you're young though, because things always turn out unbelievable. **Being in a long-term relationship … It is so beautiful.**

If you really love to spend time with someone, even if there's nothing to do, there's nothing better. The other day I had this thought – and I felt so good about myself – that if it is love, the person is there for you even if you are having a terrible time. They will still be there. Even if I'm swearing my head off or bawling my eyes out! **Everything seems better.**

Now I realize there's no point in wanting things so badly and worrying before it's the right time for you to have it.

I still have my own life, but things have this extra **shine**

16
RGS

NAME: GENEVIEVE "WEAVE" NECK
D.O.B: 03.01.73
AGE: 31 YEARS OLD
NATIONALITY: AUSTRALIAN
LIVES: SYDNEY, AUSTRALIA
OCCUPATION: FASHION / COSTUME DESIGNER

HER STORY:

I met Weave and her seven-year-old daughter, Chaquira, at her Surry Hills loft-style factory in Sydney, which she shares with a music producer and another fashion designer. Weave, a fresh-faced costume and fashion designer, has recently been doing the on-stage wardrobe for shows such as UK Idol among other things. Her eponymous Hip Hop label, "Cyberthief", is her first love, however, and she has a small but dedicated following for the edgy club-scene clothing that has become her trademark. We talked while we were on the road in California, and Las Vegas, Nevada, and back in Sydney.

A country girl at heart, Weave's amazing journey from the world of thoroughbred bloodlines to the urban underground Hip Hop clubland scene is a classic. With a depth of character that can be found only in a person who has seen and been through a lot, Weave is one of those soft touch people who loves other people and gets her kicks from anything creative that anyone is doing. Weave is the sort of person who is always to be found wherever there's a buzz. She lights up a room with her presence and is always excited to see you. The type of girl who gives props when they're due, Weave is deserving of hers.

CHAQUIRA'S EVERYTHING
I NEED! I FIND THERE ARE
NOT MANY GUYS THAT
CAN HANDLE A WOMAN
LIKE ME, BECAUSE I AM
SO HEADSTRONG AND
INDEPENDENT AND FOCUSED
ON MY CAREER AND MY CHILD.

'M ACCEPTING WHATEVER DESTINY HAS IN STORE FOR ME, BUT I'M ON A PARTICULAR PATH AT THE MOMENT THAT IS MORE SOLO.

I grew up in South Australia, in the Adelaide foothills, in the country. It's so amazingly beautiful there – it's very serene. We had a beautiful big old house and we raised thoroughbred horses – for racing. It was picture perfect, one of those really gorgeous upbringings. So I feel very priviledged that I had the opportunity to experience something that was so intensely beautiful. Because that was taken away from us completely when I was a teenager. I've had all these contrasts in my life: from where I've had beauty to being thrust into all these situations where I have had nothing at all and no support.

I lost a baby sister when she died of cot death [Sudden Infant Death Syndrome]. It shook up my family much more than we ever talk about. My mother never had any support, so she had to deal with it on her own. But it affected all of us in different ways. **WE HAVE NEVER REALLY TALKED ABOUT THE PAIN AND THE TRAGEDY OF GOING THROUGH THAT.** We all dealt with it as best we could, but it was hard for us to understand. Each person in my family pretty much went in our own directions after that, just trying to deal with it.

Another baby was born after me, a new younger sister. Naturally, my mother focused on the new baby and we felt left out and alienated I guess. But my mother had to – she was in so much pain, still dealing with the loss of a child. Because it was something that people didn't talk about at that time, she was so alone. My older sister is my strongest link to a mother figure. I mean getting a bra and boyfriends and all that stuff, Mum wasn't able to deal with it – she had deep issues due to what had happened to her. So I relied on my older sister for that sort of info. She had to go and deal with her problems by herself.The splitting up of the family happened when my father left. He started a new relationship.

Now that I have a child I understand patience and what it takes to be a parent, to be a mother. I mean finally, after twenty years, I'm just getting a handle on what the loss must have meant to my mother. And we are starting to build a really good relationship again, and it's timely because we both want to do it. It's time to forgive and to let go of the past. Being able to accept that whatever has happened in the past is in the past and it's letting go of pain and knowing and feeling that you can love again. **That has been the most difficult challenge of my life really.**

Knowing that through all the adversity that you can rise above that. That's a really major issue in turning into and becoming a woman, leaving the grassroots behind and moving into the future. I finally moved to Sydney when I was eighteen. I went to boarding school when I was twelve and I've never sort of lived with my parents after that, only for a brief period. The progression from that was I became a very independent person, individual. **JUST A LONER BASICALLY.** But before that even, it was just me and my horse! We became the best of friends and spent our day running away on a new adventure.

And – now that I think about it – it started the whole moving thing that I have in my life. **I constantly move, I constantly try new things.** I'm not afraid of anything. Whatever is placed in front of me, I'll do my best to challenge it.

MY LABEL "CYBER-THIEF" IS MY DREAM – IT'S MY HEART, MY SOUL, MY LIFE, IT'S EVERYTHING TO ME. I'D NEVER GIVE IT UP. I'M DOING IT FOR ME AND CHAQUIRA.

Koolism
9-3.30
Club
warehouse
events
Hip Hop at the Sydney Writers' Festival
Where
When
How much
More information
2003 COLOUR CARD
GOLD
JAFFA
CHOCOLATE

At ten years old, I would do these massive cross-country rides, quite alone on a big thoroughbred, but I had no fear. And I feel like that was the basis of who I am today, and why. It was all because of my beautiful horse and my childhood and upbringing in that place.

I need to sell my clothes, so America is important as the primary Hip Hop market. Nothing is about me any more, once you have a child, it's not the same. You have to do everything possible to get ahead. Because I have Chaquira, I strive so much harder to make things work. If you don't have children, I don't know if you strive as hard. When you don't take responsibility like that, it's kind of okay to just plod along, and there's not as much pressure to succeed.

I grew up in a very "white" society I guess. A lot of free settlers went to South Australia as opposed to convicts, as in the rest of Australia. It was a total hierarchy, compared to the rest of Australia. It was so incredibly different for me when I went to the city. At boarding school it was the first time I saw racially different people. When I was seventeen, I left home and went to fashion school. I felt that there was so much more to life.

It was an instinctive thing, I knew there was so much more I needed to complete in my life. I moved to Sydney to go to fashion school. I live in Bondi now and I get so excited to meet people from different cultures. I love hearing a new person's story and their background.

The video clips for Hip Hop that are shown in the mainstream are filthy as a general rule. They degrade the notion of Hip Hop, which is storytelling. But again, it's different in different plces - Australian Hip Hop guys wouldn't create video clips of rappers slapping women's butts close-up in camera! It simply doesn't happen. That is something that is peculiar to American Hip Hop. And women in general dress differently there.

America is such a strange place. We were walking past signs that said "dirty girls, cold beer". It's such a strange perception that men have about women there. I don't understand it at all. All the plastic surgery that people have! Why do people have to produce themselves more and more? To make themselves real. But that's sad. Why can't people just roll with who they are? I'm having a hard time trying to understand it all!

I'm not trying to fit in there, because I know I never will, but I can't understand why people have to try so hard to become something that they're not. I've seen women that looked completely and utterly bizarre. At a beach night club, they were dancing in the pool and on the pontoons in g-strings! All the dancers were white as well. It was reverse racism, and that happens a lot in the States. We had a lot of comments - that were racially directed, which amazed me, I'm not used to that, coming from Sydney where we are all so mixed.

Youth culture and drug culture seem to go hand-in-hand. And that's a global thing. I don't think it's confined to any one country. At one particular party I went to in the States they were handing out shots of liquid cocaine. It's readily available, that's for sure. I can't say I have ever been offered it in Australia. Heroin is so big in Australia. It's everywhere, it's in your face and it's a big issue with the government. Cocaine seems to be more the thing in America.

Chaquira's everything I need! I found love once with Chaquira's father, and I think that's a very rare thing. That doesn't happen very often. I haven't found it again, but I know it will happen again for me, but just not yet, and I may have another child.

I'm accepting whatever destiny has in store for me, but I'm on a particular path at the moment that is more solo. And I know there are lots of little alleys you can go down along the way. I split up with Chaquira's father two years ago. He was my first love. When we met I was twenty-two and he was nineteen. I had Chaquira when I was twenty-three. A lot of people think that when you're young and having a child that it was a mistake … We were together for eight years – it was a significant long-term relationship. We planned on having her and we were so in love. We were so happy and for a long time too. He came into my life and made everything solid. He brought a lot of stability into it … He was my angel. But people change and if you don't move in the same circles any more, you can have a lot of conflict, so that can be hard.

We talk about getting back together all the time. We are still very close. We let the relationship take whatever form is necessary for us to grow. I NEED TO FOCUS ON MY SOUL.

In a serious relationship - which I really believe in - you grow together and you do things, but eventually you do grow apart. I thought I was going to be with my man forever at that stage when I was twenty-two. We met, fell in love, had a baby and thought that everything was going to be beautiful forever. And then … we grew up! We realized that we were both changing and have a lot of stuff to do in our lives. You don't want to hold yourself back from doing things in your life because of a relationship. **A LOT OF MY FRIENDS DON'T BELIEVE IN MARRIAGE AT ALL. THAT'S BECAUSE WE ALL THINK THAT MARRIAGE PROPOSES AN IDEAL THAT'S NOT POSSIBLE. IT'S UNATTAINABLE.** If I ever regain my trust in men again, then perhaps I'll change my opinion. Trust is a really big thing and when you've been hurt in your life, you take it really seriously.

I'm so glad that I had my child, because I feel like I was put on this earth to do something special and I've done the major part of that now, in reproducing. She saved me! She brought my family together. She's been the one that created the depth to my life. I thank God or the angels that I did that and at that time. And I'm glad that I never got married, because divorce is so hard for children to go through. Because we didn't have to go through the legalities of it all, my partner and I were able to deal with the breakup in a mature, calm way. We are very close and we spend a lot of time together still. We are still a family. But my ex-partner is a very special person, he is one in a million.

I believe that everybody is in charge of their own destiny. We are not here purely as pleasure articles for men. We all have our own choices. Those girls who are doing that - well, it is their choice. I'm in no position to be stopping people from their destiny, whatever that is. I'm not turning a blind eye to it, because it certainly exists, and it will always be there, however I choose not to be involved with it. I try to focus on me and my own positivity and what I want out of life. As they are doing - they must be doing it because they like it. That doesn't mean it doesn't affect me negatively.

My destiny, my soul and who I am, that's all developing very strongly and it has done so for the past couple of years … But I need this time. This is soul-work time for me. But it can never be all about me ever again. Chaquira is a part of me forever.

NEXT TIME I GO I'M GONNA ROCK THAT PLACE!!!
I feel like the whole world has just opened for me! **Mum's going to be so proud.**

BUBBLY
BRIGHT
FUN
CARING
DREAMY
SIMPLE
HARD WORKING
SMILING

♥ Jo

RGS

NAME: LYNDA-JANE "LJ" SHAFER
D.O.B: 23.03.85
AGE: 19 YEARS OLD
NATIONALITY: AUSTRALIAN
LIVES: NEWCASTLE, AUSTRALIA
OCCUPATION: ASSISTANT EVENT COORDINATOR

HER STORY

How I came to know LJ is one of those unusual sequence of events that you could in no way correlate the chances of nor the nature of the outcome. I began chatting to her mother, Lyn Shafer, and we got to talking about life. As these things turn out, we ended up talking about the week we were both having. My grandmother had just died and my grandfather and father were both admitted into hospital - all in the space of a week. As it turned out her family had recently had a similar run and we were both literally shaking our heads at how things happen. Then she told me about her daughter LJ. I sent them both some books and a friendship was born.

LJ is probably the person for whom the word "bubbly" was invented. There is no other way to describe her! She's a highly articulate and bright young thing who will go on to do great things in life. Compassionate and aware of the opportunities before her, LJ aims high but she still loves the simple things in life. What else can you say about **a gorgeous girl whose favorite color is pink, "because it's a bright, fun color", who loves the beach, "it's my escape", and whose favorite food is chocolate cake, "'cos it soothes the soul"?**

I was born in Newcastle in New South Wales. You know what they say: Born smarter in the Mater![Mater Hospital]. [laughs] I have an older brother. With Mum and Dad, the four of us are really close. We've been through a lot together. We're a team. Whatever bad things come, we face together. I still live at home.

In my first year out of school I went to business college and I graduated at the end of 2003. I received a Diploma of Business Management. It's been an experience, because I have been so focused on my studies – and I had my best and worst time all in the one period of my life. **I was down but I was very motivated. Bizarre! I was awarded the New South Wales Young Achievement Australia Business Person of the Year.**

That put me on a high!

Whenever there is a family crisis we bond. We had a stage where everything happened at once – a death in the family, relationship breakups, my brother moved out, my father became redundant at work. I never imagined living without my Pop, my Mum's father. He was such a thorough gentleman. But now I know death is a fact and I have learned to accept change. They were the tough times, but they seem minute now!

The defining moment of my childhood was when I went to high school and met new people. I began to understand that not everyone is the same and that everyone goes through changes. I moved on from some of my old friends, met new ones and began to develop my direction. I began to put positive energy into myself.

I pretty much live each day to the fullest – you never know what's around the corner – and I try not to have any regrets – anything in life whether it appears to be a good or a bad thing, is a learning experience. I have proof! I broke up my relationship. I was totally in love and pretty much devoted my whole life to that relationship and to my boyfriend. But I was still only eighteen and it was too much. You can only move forward, you can't go back.

I am definitely single at the moment. It was my boyfriend's decision initially to break up our two-year relationship, but we could both see it coming, but we ignored it because we were both so in love with each other. It was in the end more like a mutual agreement. There was a lot of pain on both sides at first.

But despite that, I am happy the way things have turned out as much as I couldn't see it at the time. I was a mess. Poor Mum, she was really beginning to stress about me. I was holding onto it with a little string and I didn't want to let go of the attachment, I was obsessing and it wasn't healthy. Breaking up made me realize that I didn't need a relationship to survive. The breakup taught me to be stronger on my own and to discover who I really was as an individual. The "I" in me became "him and me" over the two years and I wasn't an individual any more, he was part of everything I did and it was too much. In the end, you just have to know that the time isn't right. **Now I know I have to live my dreams and not someone else's. I think I've had my time as a committed person, now it's ME time!**

MY PERSONAL PHILOSOPHY

Discover my purpose in life, always be true to myself as well as others!

Learn from my mistakes & never live life with regrets!

To continue dreaming & do everything I can to make those dreams come true!

Balance a healthy life of work & fun!

Learn to love myself before I can love anyone else!

To be forever happy & to SMILE always!

LJ

The breakup was a positive, awesome experience. It defined me and made me realize who I am.

I was going to move to the city, have kids, the usual stuff – everything was "mapped out". Now I'm more open to decision making on my own and enjoying the freedom (and the fear!) in that. I have so much life ahead of me. You need to do what you want to do. As a kid, I always dreamed I would travel, now I'm making travel plans!

I always wanted to work in tourism – in events or marketing – and I have recently started working as an Assistant Event Coordinator, so I have taken my first step towards my dream. I also dream of helping the youth of today. I think as a teenager I needed help and guidance – a neutral sounding board to help you realize that when you're young in life, things can get scary but that everything will be okay. Each person needs to find a reason for being here. We need to cut down on the suicide rates and drug use **and teach people how to live a natural, fun life.**

I want a pretty traditional life I guess, eventually. But while I'm young and not tied down I want to experience travel – by myself. I would like to be comfortable and not have to struggle through life. I don't mean just in money terms, but I don't want to struggle with emotions either. A lot of people will get married just so they can live the so-called ideal life. They don't know how to do it as themselves.

As much as people like to think they're perfect, as a couple you need to compromise on faults. I don't think you should change for someone. **You can be the team that is "unbreakable" but it is a compromise, it's not a one-way street.**

I believe in marriage, but I believe in divorce too.

But there are so many things that need to change in society. Society should accept that men can be depressed and not coping. Men are still not allowed to admit or be seen to have any weakness. It is seen as pretty much a female thing, but that has to change. I don't think society has developed the correct support systems or if they exist they are not being marketed properly. There is no encouragement to come out and be open about what you're going through financially, emotionally or whatever.

And right now, guys are being stereotyped to want that "ideal" chick. And they are stereotyped to just want sex. We have to explain and educate young men about the real issues around pornography. Like most women, I get intimidated by pornography and how women are represented in men's magazines. People don't realize how dangerous it is – it's not healthy. If men stopped and looked properly, they would see that it's fake. It stops women being who they are. And then you are looked at by guys as a kind of shadow, as if there's someone in front of you that they want you to be. So that's the message that the girls get subconsciously. **And then they start to think, I'm not good enough, I've got to change to fit that ideal.** So that's where it all starts.

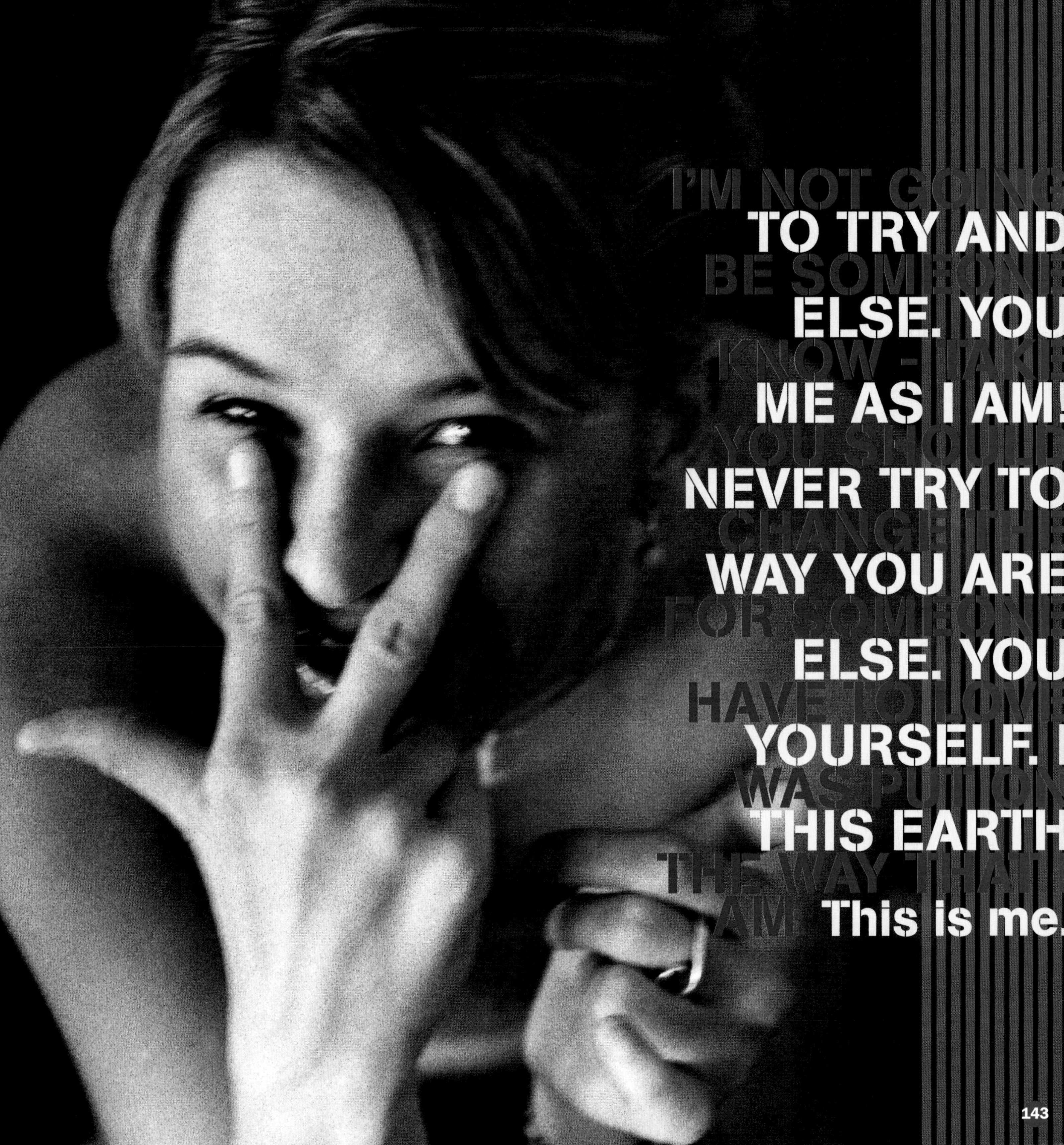

I'M NOT GOING
TO TRY AND
BE SOMEONE
ELSE. YOU
KNOW - TAKE
ME AS I AM!
YOU SHOULD
NEVER TRY TO
CHANGE THE
WAY YOU ARE
FOR SOMEONE
ELSE. YOU
HAVE TO LOVE
YOURSELF. I
WAS PUT ON
THIS EARTH
THE WAY THAT I
AM. This is me.

Romy Campbell is in transition – the ultimate place to observe and reflect upon things for anyone. And there is plenty to reflect upon, for Romy has had one of the most adventurous (and certainly one of the most unusual) work and lifestyles of anyone I know. When I finally caught up with her after a long period of being out of touch, I discovered that Romy had changed gears. The earthy and pioneering camel leader I first met is now a student and city-based. For several years on a remote stretch of the Western Australian coast, Romy catered for tourists and backpackers with her own brand of laidback thrills, and carved out a niche business at a young age. Strong, adaptable, capable and compassionate, Romy is one of those people who immediately impresses and inspires.

Having moved from such a blissful beach and bush-based existence to a city life early in 2004, Romy's world these days revolves around her studies in naturopathy and her goal to be a healer. But the world of the camels is never far from her mind and she still has plans to include them again at some point in her future. Ever practical, Romy has other plans that involve settling down, but as a longtime traveler she still dreams of distant places.

For hers is a gypsy name and Romy is passionate about her gypsy life. It's what she thrives on.

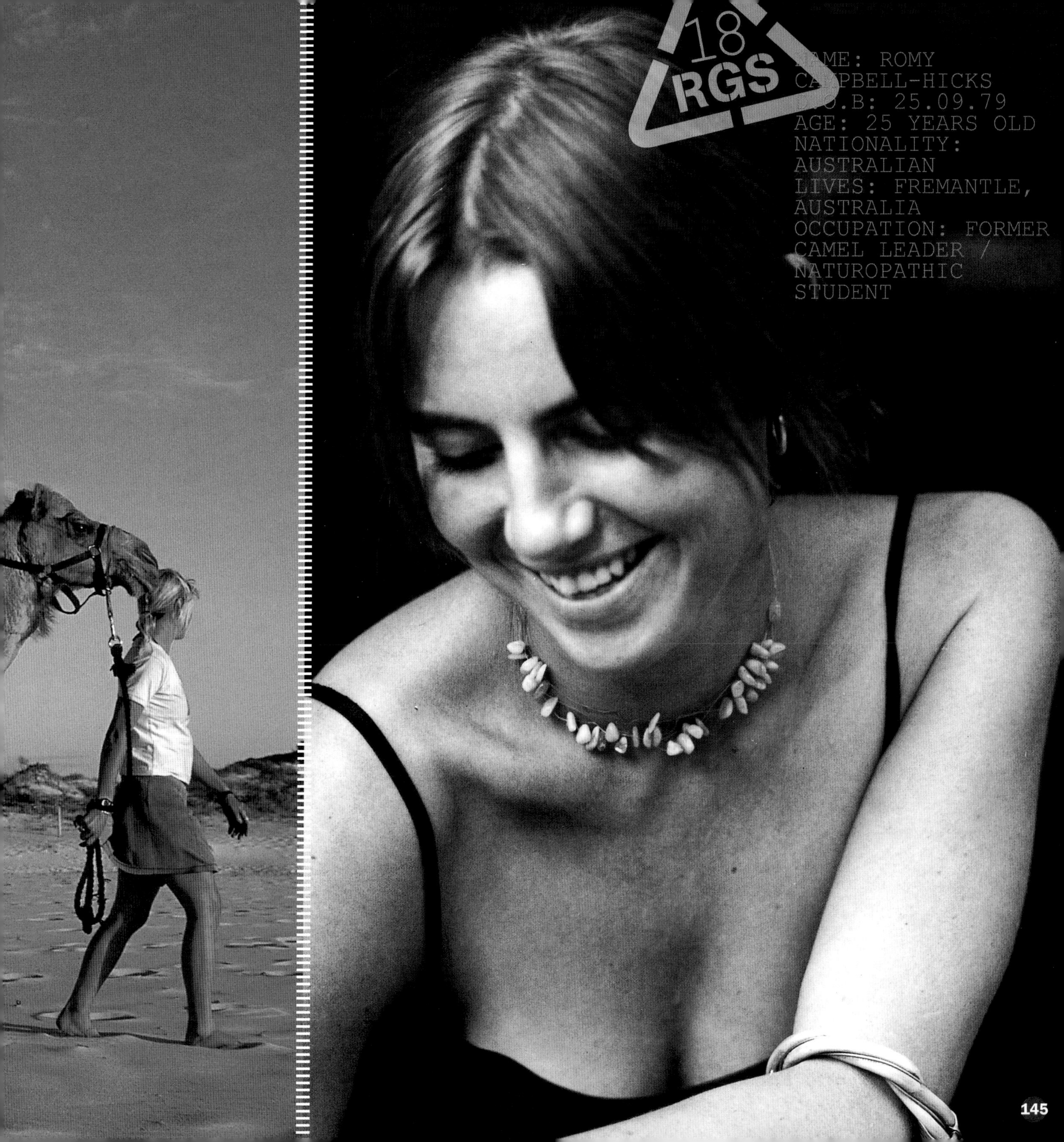
18
RGS
NAME: ROMY
CAMPBELL-HICKS
D.O.B: 25.09.79
AGE: 25 YEARS OLD
NATIONALITY:
AUSTRALIAN
LIVES: FREMANTLE,
AUSTRALIA
OCCUPATION: FORMER
CAMEL LEADER /
NATUROPATHIC
STUDENT

PRACTICAL MYSTICAL
CAPABLE COMPASSIONATE
LAIDBACK HIPPY CHICK
GYPSY ADVENTUROUS
HEALER ADAPTABLE STRONG

PEOPLE TRIP OUT ON WHAT I'VE DONE. I THINK THEY FIND IT HARD TO BELIEVE I USED TO RUN THE CAMEL SAFARIS. NOW BEING UP IN THE CITY I FEEL SO FAR AWAY FROM IT... BUT IT'S STILL SUCH A PART OF ME AND WHO I AM.

I come from a small closeknit family, consisting of my parents and my younger brother. I grew up in southwest Western Australia on Binningup Beach [Note:"up" means "waterhole" in Aboriginal] about three and a half hours from Perth.

We grew up in the country but we also had the beach lifestyle. There's so much energy there! I love the blend of nature and people and space. It's what makes where we live so unique. Dad traveled a lot as a gold miner. He started off working in mines in Western Australia, but within ten years he was being sent to places like Botswana and Ghana [in Africa], Russia, Canada, Papua New Guinea, Turkey... so we had been around the world a lot before I left home at seventeen. When I was eleven my mother took me and my little brother, who was nine at the time, around Europe backpacking by ourselves. We were in traveling school! I lived in the United Kingdom for a year near Hereford, near Wales. I went to school in Wales for a year, when I was twelve.

Instead of going camping - as most children from where I lived would do - we would be going to visit my father somewhere in the world. I think it gave me broader horizons and as a result I thought bigger and beyond - where others might see limitations. I saw so much variety through traveling that I naturally had a bigger picture in my mind for life in general. It also gave me an inner confidence to travel by myself, so then I went to Switzerland on an exchange for three months and then, [of my own accord] I took myself to England and got a job. I wasn't trying to go home. It was normal for me to keep going and traveling. I had relatives there but I stayed in London for four months before going on a holiday to Portugal before returning home.

I was eighteen when I bought the camel safari business. Got a loan and I had guarantors. I had the opportunity to do that early which was fortunate. And my family was incredibly supportive. I have always been very appreciative and grateful for that.

I came back having experienced so much overseas and I had no idea what I was going to do. I enrolled in a business degree at Edith Cowan University in Bunbury. I wanted something broad that would help with a lot of jobs. I didn't know what I wanted to specialize in so I thought I would do something general in business. I was being practical! I had been at university for about six months. I was looking for land, just dreaming and browsing.

I was looking at a local paper at the breakfast table at my Mum's house and we flicked open Businesses for Sale. There was an ad that said "Four Friendly Camels need a new home. Change your life. Make an Offer". He was a businessman who had bought the business but he didn't know what to do with it. My Mum was the catalyst. She said to me, "You can do this!" Her encouragement made all the difference to being in the frame of mind to take it on. She

Romy

MY NAME, ROMY, IS A GYPSY NAME AND I REALLY RELATE TO THAT WHOLE GYPSY FLOW, THE TRAVELING AROUND THING. I REALLY LOVE IT.

I think about how my life has changed since I was sitting at that kitchen table! Interestingly, I had to have the passion to do it, it wasn't about the money in the end. I just did it for the love. I didn't make any money at all but hanging out with these camels was amazing – being in the outdoors, putting smiles on faces was enough! Business is not just about money. It's more about love. It's a really good example when you've got animals. It doesn't matter what it costs, you have to get along with them, love them, look after them and do whatever it takes really.

When I bought the business it was called West Coast Camels & Co., but I re-named it Yallingup Camel Safaris. I had ridden camels before as a kid, but I had no experience with large animals of any kind. But in a way that was a good thing, because I was open to everything in the beginning. I had to learn everything from scratch and through experience. I had a friend who was sixteen and she came to help me. And while she had a bit of horse experience, it wasn't all that relevant! We talked to a lot of camel owners to learn the ropes. We also learned that camel owners are all slightly eccentric in some way!

The fear was definitely there when I started, but it dissipated pretty fast! I had to learn so much that I had more to focus on than the fear and it turns around pretty quickly with camels because you're their master, so you have to take it on. When I was learning it was a bit one-on-one, they were testing me and I was testing them. There came a shift. If you treat them well, then they're going to work for you well in return. Same for humans really. Camels aren't known for being submissive. They would let you know if you weren't treating them well. It's especially clear when you work with animals, they let you know straightaway if you're being fair with them or not.

It's so easy to make people happy through the camels!

I started the business with eight camels. Two camels - one adult and a calf - died early on because they had not been looked after properly. At one point there were ten, but then I sold a couple. It's called a herd or a caravan [when they travel as a troupe]: Camellia, Madison, Shah, Alabaster "Ali", Jamal, Heidi, Kimba, Sharon, Shan, Digger.

I used to do sunset rides at Smiths Beach – the most beautiful, long beach with pristine sand and crazy sunsets. It's really special and perfect for long rides. I'd take the whole lot down there. Two adults and a calf in the trailer. It looked so funny because the camels' heads would stick out of the top of the trailer and the Land Cruiser. So I would do bush rides in winter, beach and sunset rides in summer and all the festivals.

It was hard work and really long hours. **YOU HAD TO BE ON-CALL TWENTY-FOUR HOURS A DAY, SEVEN DAYS A WEEK.** One time I had to look after a new-born calf and bottle feed it three times a day. Madison, his mother, neglected him after she gave birth to him, which happens occasionally. Before I bought the business, she had another calf and it had apparently died and she was really upset. I think that had something to do with her rejecting this one. Camel babies need their mother's milk within forty-eight hours of being born or their immune system doesn't develop properly and they become more susceptible to infection. I wanted to do my best for him, although he was a weak baby. He was so cute though. He was a mixture of human and calf because he was around humans so much.

Anyhow, it went on for a couple of months without any improvement. I had a roster of people to help me out but I almost had a nervous breakdown. I was getting no sleep and I was seriously stressed. It felt like I had a child, but with this bizarre edge, as I'd have to drive out to a paddock in the middle of the night, to look after this "child". It was the heaviest thing when he died and I was devastated at the time. That was the emotional part of the business.

Just after I sold the business Madison died. She ate some baler twine [wrapped up bales of hay]. Hearing about her death was one of the hardest things, however I had disconnected from them at that point and there was really nothing I could do.

But there were many happy times too. The best memories were when I used to go to festivals. I loved doing events with the camels. You'd rock up to a location, see heaps of people, make your money for the day and move on.

My biggest goal when I finish my course is to do a long camel journey. My mother's sister – and my namesake aunt – Romy, is a camel lover, and she wants to do a big trip across Australia too. She is a huge inspiration, mentor and a real adventurer. She is a survivor too – she's been on team expeditions to the North Pole! She's now fifty-two, has a career as a management consultant and has never married. She's a gypsy like me!

I got engaged in October 2003 and that would probably be my best memory from the past ten years. I have been with my boyfriend, Adima, for three years. We were having a sunset picnic at one of our favorite beaches – beautiful circumstances – and we were having this conversation about past lives. We were just looking at each other and then he came out with it! We give each other what we need. We don't have dates yet, we'll do it when it feels right – maybe next year when we've settled into Perth a bit more. **It feels so easy and right. I think we were meant to be together.**

It's taken a while to settle into the city, it's very different from the country … I know why I am here – I have good reasons to be here. Being in the city is a huge change from the country where I have lived for most of my life. Through studying I am becoming more focused and aware of things because now I have a comparison between the two. I've had to find some new interests and work out what my old interests were. I realized that I have missed the ocean and things like surfing. Because it's all completely new in the city. I've had to find the good beaches again and learn where the dance classes are held. Everything is new for me.

IT'S BEEN A BIG CHANGE THOUGH AND I'VE HAD TO WORK OUT WHO I AM AGAIN

I HAVEN'T FORGOTTEN MY OTHER DREAMS AND MY OTHER GOALS.

When I lived down south I did fire twirling performances and belly dancing performances, which I loved. I got together with a couple of girls I knew and we called ourselves "Earth Sisters". We were approached by another friend to do the Earth Dance for World Peace. This is a world party that goes on in about twenty countries around the world, at the same time, in every time zone. There is a prayer that is said after the performance of the dance and everyone holds hands and says it. We have also been approached by something called "Conscious Living", which is a holistic annual festival held in Perth in November. We have done it a few times now, but each time we do the dance, it changes slightly according to what or whom we are dancing for.

It is a dance that is based on the chakras – from the Hindu belief system. It's a blend of Tai Chi mixed with belly dancing, Sufi dancing and, of course, Indian dancing. Every move we make has some influence. I like using a lot of energy from the earth. It's often an instinctive thing, and we use the ground itself in the movements. We even pick up handfuls of dirt! Breathing throughout is important. It's a dancing meditation.

I'm studying the Advanced Diploma of Naturopathy and Herbalism at a private university called The Herbal Farm. It's a comprehensive, four-year course and I'm in the first year. It's so positive! And it's so good for me too. I'm learning the basics at the moment, but I look forward to being able to heal people in a positive way. More than ever people are looking for non-invasive ways to heal. I'm interested in it for my own life but then I want to share what I've learned with other people. I imagine it's something I'll use in my personal world, on family and friends, and of course if I was to go and work with camels again...

Right now I am putting my heart and soul into my course. But at the same time I'm still enjoying my life and being with my partner. **I WOULD LOVE TO DO A FULL-BLOWN CAMEL EXPEDITION AND GET SPONSORS AND COVERAGE AND SO FORTH.** **The energy is still growing for that, and that would take about a year to plan. After the camel expedition, I'd love to have a family.**

Living somewhere is always different to traveling through or visiting. I needed to move to the city – even though it'd been so hard to say goodbye to the camels. I needed to do it for myself and I'm learning a whole range of life skills that I didn't even know about. For instance, now I'm wary that there are strange people out there. That wasn't so real to me before as I have never come across anyone whom I couldn't trust. I'm learning to look out for myself, safety-wise. I was too naive in the city. Unfortunately you can't trust everyone.

CURIOUS
passionate
CREATIVE
SOULFUL BRAVE
COURAGEOUS
RISKTAKER (NOT ALWAYS
CALCULATED) SOMETIMES
Spontaneous
OFF-THE-WALL
VIBRANT
QUIRKY
FABULOUS (of course!)

NAME: PETRINA EDGE

D.O.B: 01.06.79

AGE: 25 YEARS OLD

NATIONALITY: AUSTRALIAN

LIVES: SYDNEY, AUSTRALIA

OCCUPATION: ACTOR / RETAIL ASSISTANT

HER STORY:

I first met Petrina when she wrote to me after one of my books was published. We struck up an ongoing correspondence and one day agreed to meet. She came into the café wearing a flowing lavender printed chiffon top and tons of jewelry – the full inner-city boho princess – and she was just so excited about everything. From the moment Petrina entered the room I could sense there was something about her that was wildly different. We talked about all sorts of things that day, and the following week she even came to help me sort out my massive photo archive for a short time, just before she was cast in a reality television series.

One of the first things that strikes you about Petrina – apart from her obvious outgoing nature – is her fearlessness. She is one of the most deeply passionate people I have met. Petrina is always so animated – it's understandable why her chosen craft is acting – and at the same time she can be surprisingly and quietly sanguine. It's an interesting combination. I always think her last name says a lot about her, because she is often taking risks and testing herself – she likes to go out on the edge. I love that about her! Petrina has a lot of worldly smarts and the mettle to take on things most people could never – and would never – dream about pulling off. It is one of her best qualities, of which there are many.

I was born in Gosford on the Central Coast of new South Wales, Australia. I spent my childhood on the coast and my adolescence in the west of Sydney. My mother is from Malta, and my grandparents migrated after the Second World War – two of their children were born in Malta and the other three were born in Australia. My Mum's family have a home in the Fairfield area.

Fairfield is the most culturally diverse city in the country. I did a project on it in high school. There are eighty-nine different nationalities in the area – this was a few years ago, so it may be a slightly different figure – and it represents almost every religion. There will be a Buddhist temple on one side of the street, and churches of every sort nearby, or on the other side of the street. I came from the central coast to that! It was a major culture shock at ten years old. I didn't really understand - not until much later in life - **my ethnicity.**

If you look at my school photographs, I was one of three kids with dark hair! I think we had one grade 4 student from Japan though, and he was like a novelty to us as little kids. When I first saw an Asian child – and this was in the mid-eighties – I couldn't believe it.

But **basically I was the only one who wasn't blond.** Though when you go to the Central Coast these days, it's completely different.

Fairfield was a total shock! Based on my appearance, people probably thought I'd be comfortable there. But I hadn't come from that - I hadn't experienced that kind of diversity at all. But it didn't take long for that to change and I soon enjoyed it all. My high school photos were a complete reversal of my primary school ones … there is the occasional blond-haired person!

I got a position with the Multi-cultural Theatre Alliance for Carnivale in Sydney in 2000. It was a project - a play - in which I had an acting role. It was called "Insomnia" and it featured six different writers from ethnic backgrounds telling six stories. In three of the stories I was cast as two Lebanese girls and in one story I played a Spanish girl. Through my acting I've learned how to embrace my ethnicity. The play "Insomnia" was my awakening.

I have been taken for almost every nationality you can think of. I feel very Australian, but I'm aware of the difference between me and the typical Australian – or of what is portrayed as the typical Australian female in the media. **I don't fit into the myth** of what that is supposed to be. It's still a pretty narrow definition, even today. But what we have become is what we're learning to embrace more. If I am traveling and someone asks me where I come from, they are always surprised if I say I am Australian. The Crocodile Dundee myth is alive and well overseas! And the reality is washed over by the global myth of what is Australia, who are Australians and what it is to live here. There is an Aboriginal awareness, but it's a bit like most people being dimly aware of Native Americans living in America.

If we don't have a grasp here on who it is we are and what we stand for, then how can we represent that internationally in any fashion, beyond existing cultural myths? Australia is a young country, so we are still in the process of defining that.

RINA

Politically, it is a very important time. We now have a fully functioning country, however the position we take with respect to the world is very undecided. **What sort of consciousness do we have as a country?** That's why everybody is struggling so much – it's a bit like having all the ingredients to make a cake but no recipe. We need an Australian Jamie Oliver to bake it! Our current political leaders might have a bit to learn in the kitchen – I'm not sure their culinary skills are quite up to scratch!

The refugee issue is a complex one, but **I'm definitely not into putting up barriers.** Barriers create isolation. They don't aid or assist development. Assimilation, integration, diversification … who cares? What you want is harmony.

I don't prescribe to a religion per se, although I was baptised Catholic. However, I never went to a Catholic school and I never went to church. My family didn't attach themselves to Catholicism. My Mum's not religious. The Maltese community is traditionally hard-core fundamentalist Catholic. I would describe my grandparents as traditional though. Grandma died when I was three years old, and I think the religious aspect was more a function of being a part of the community. I have never regarded religion in that formal way, although I have investigated Buddhism and Hinduism.

I believe in God or some sort of higher power. But that to me in a practical sense means listening to my own instincts. The universe is land and people at a core level. And if I believe anything it's a universal wisdom – and a wisdom of the heart.

I did fairly well at school but I was a bit rebellious and more interested in seeing bands and partying. In recent times I have wondered how I would have done if I'd applied myself. I was thirteen or fourteen and itching for the world to come to my feet – or to go out and meet the world! I felt restricted by my environment. I wanted more than I felt I could have – what seemed to be or what I perceived to be available.

As a child I was curious about the world. From a pretty young age I had an inquiry into life and its deeper meanings. I was looking for some sort of meaning and purpose and some way to understand it. And **I was never satisfied** with the answers of the people around me. That sent me on my own journey into the world.

A really key issue for young women — and maybe this is oversimplifying things — is the issue **of self-esteem.** This issue manifests itself in eating disorders, boredom, excessive eating, and binge drinking on weekends. The umbrella issue for all of these things is really self-esteem. It is related to all aspects of how young women think and feel about themselves. They are faced with internal and external issues.

What's not often mentioned in regard to self-esteem, is that it can be lowered or **eroded by boredom.** Each of us needs to learn to be creative and to make creativity a way of life. There are creative aspects to a career path, but there also has to be creativity for your own wellbeing and growth, and general stimulation and inspiration. Developing skills is great for self-esteem. **It's for your Self!** Skills and knowledge are power. By power I mean as in self-empowerment, which is the exact key to overcoming depression. Nobody who feels depressed doesn't feel disempowered in some way.

you can't make any change happen until you are actually willing to do it

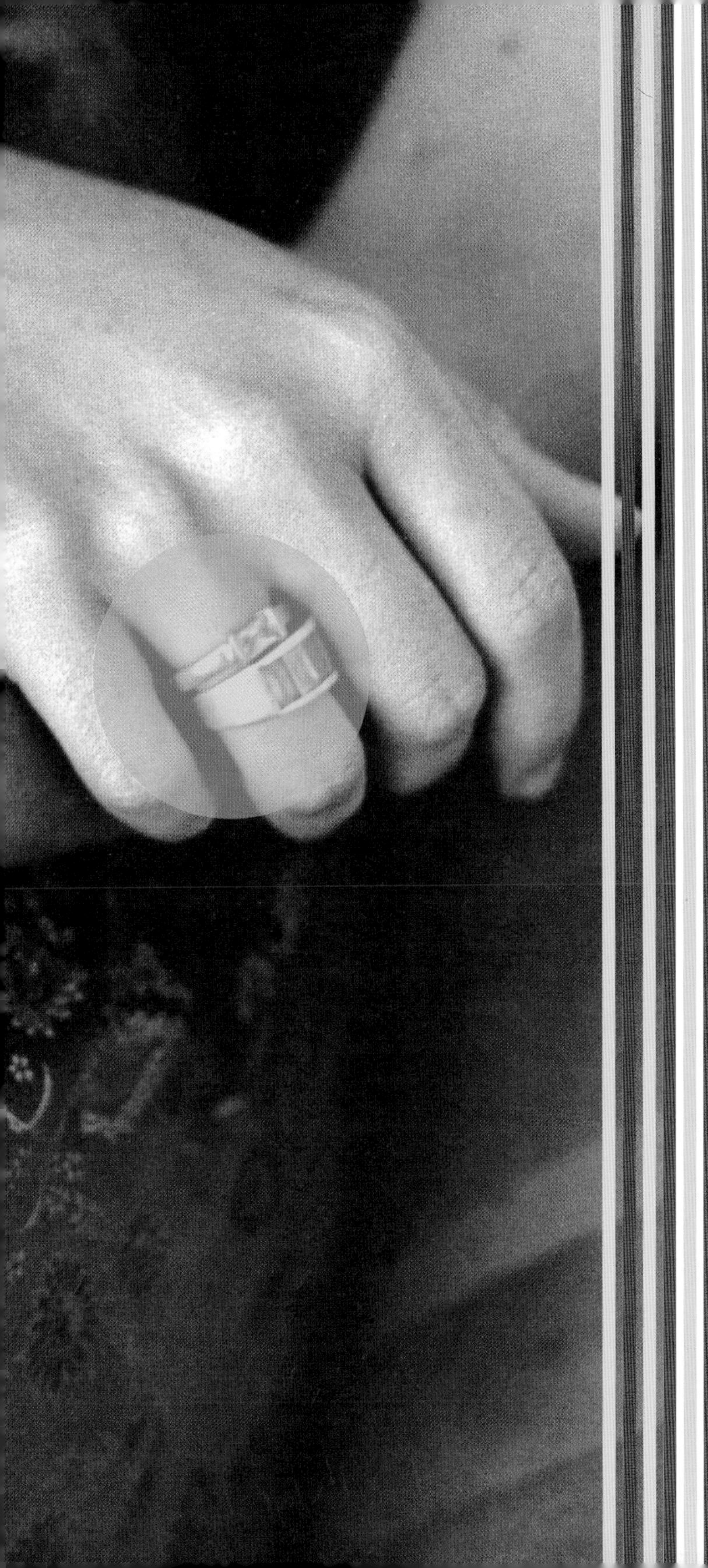

It helps people to get a sense of their own capabilities, value and worth. Anything that does that, fosters creativity and therefore confidence. Having just returned from overseas I have found it is too easy to become idle. I'm not working much and I'm not acting at the moment. Lack of activity leads to an idle mind. And **an idle mind leads to negativity.** It's easy to get stuck and become stuck in a rut of mundane nothingness.

The best and the worst news is that no one is going to do it for you! Knowing isn't enough. **You have to act.**

I have been involved with a self-help organization in the past. And they had a saying "The Universe rewards action". It's a nice thing to remember! You can't make any change happen until you're actually willing to do it. And once you do something you get immediate feedback and support as soon as you do. I've integrated this to a certain level. And now I have to go to another one.

Your own heart knows what is best for you in the moment. You have to have the courage to follow your own wisdom. Nobody else knows what's right for you but you.

When I need inspiration I go for a run, go to the beach, yoga, meditation, writing in my journal. I **don't have a hard and fast rule about anything.** I was vegan for a while, until it wasn't working for me anymore. I go on whatever feels right in the moment. Different things work at different times, for different people … And you just have to know it for yourself.

Service is a great way to build self-esteem. It keeps you humble. In *The Prophet* by Khalil Gibran, he writes that the true nature of giving is to give without expectation. That's unconditionality in action!

I did a community theater project in Thailand. I was there for seven weeks and the project took three weeks. I wanted to go overseas, and to travel in Southeast Asia specifically, but I was also feeling **really creative** and so I joined this program with the Makhampom Theatre Group. I paid money to participate, as the Group was using the project as a means to raise funds. It involved working with disadvantaged groups who were mostly from rural communities, who had been ravaged by poverty and many of whom had been involved in prostitution. It really opened my eyes. We have very little comprehension of what eighty percent of the world suffers on a daily basis. I'm saying this as a statement of fact rather than of judgement. But it was an intense three weeks. The Makhampom Theatre Group use the theater as a social and political agent for change. I came away from the experience feeling really inspired and with the knowledge that theater can educate, **inspire and motivate for change** at a grassroots level.

If half the population on Earth could get together and drink a cup of tea and eat the odd quality chocolate – the world would be a better place! It's not about saving the world overnight though. It's about one on one basic interaction. This is at an achievable level and the rewards are instant.

I took on the role of "The Mole", in the [Australian] reality television show of the same name. The show is based around a competition whereby contestants earn money by completing certain physical and mental **challenges**. It was a **psychological game** in the way that one person – nicknamed The Mole – is in the guise of a contestant, but is really a saboteur. The process of elimination takes all of the ten episodes of the show. And so I was briefed to be The Mole! In general I am not a fan of reality television – I would never have sought it out and nor would I ever do it again – but I approached it as a professional acting gig. The producers have certain specific criteria that they are looking for. And I was approached the evening after I broke up a long-term relationship. So, really I was an empty canvas from day one of breaking up. I actually believe it was a blessing.

I believed I was given it because I wasn't functioning and it gave me something entirely different to focus upon. The producers drilled me – it's pretty intense psychological profiling and analysis – and they had two key things they looked for. One, the person had to be incredibly trustworthy as he/she needed to be able to **maintain secrecy**, outside the show as well. And that was six months all up of secrecy! On one of the episodes they flew a guest over to be on the show. My Dad was flown over to New Caledonia and he was playing and still didn't know that I was The Mole! And the second thing the producers were looking for when casting the role was a certain playful quality and the ability to **deceive and enjoy** that.

It was a game of deception and accordingly I looked at it as a role of deception in the same way an actor deceives an audience. The challenge was for me, as an actor, the same as any other role. **I wasn't being myself!** So as long as I kept it in that frame, I was fine with it. It's all about framing and context. I knew the people who know me and love me would understand and never see it as an issue of real deception. They saw me as doing my job, and doing it well. That's what I hoped for and that was the outcome. I mean, **[laughs]** I couldn't have guaranteed it would turn out that way!

Regrets don't cross my mind. To have regret is a funny way of looking at life. Everything has a purpose and the challenge is really to extrapolate **the lessons** as you go. The beauty of hindsight is that you can look at things and imagine how you might have done it differently, but safe in the knowledge of where you actually are. **I think of things in terms of wisdom.** Maybe I did something the hard way, then I can concede I could have made things easier for myself, **without blaming myself** or whatever. It's attitudinal and it affects your self-judgement, but it's far wiser to frame things in a positive manner. Over time I have found that if I set things up in a certain way then it totally affects how I feel about it and **ultimately how I feel** about myself.

We need to re-examine the **notion of grief**, in general, and as **a process**. I think it needs to be overhauled, in particular the things that society deems worthy of grieving for. The message often seems to be pack up, move on, leave [whatever it is] behind you and as soon as possible. However, there is a process of grieving and it's something that, particularly in the Western world, we don't know much about. It's to do with immortality.

I was quite heavily **involved in Animal Liberation** from the age of about eighteen up until I was twenty-one or twenty-two. I wrote articles for the Vegan Society. I coordinated stalls and markets at music events and festivals. I was totally hardcore about animal liberation, but I am no longer a vegan. It's been an interesting process ideologically. I still believe in minimizing suffering to animals in the world. And I am still interested in my health and wellbeing, and diet is a major part of that. I have also lately been re-assessing the application of an animal-free diet again, but to what level and how I do that is uncertain. **Traveling kind of gave me some new things to think about.** Learning about and understanding new and different cultures for instance. Food is a big part of how we do that.

I'm not into being hardcore "anything" these days. If I was into anything in the past, my approach to things was **a bit extreme when I was younger.** I'm chilling out more and I'm less intense these days. But my vegan diet in those years was an incredible spiritual awakening for me too. As you contemplate the treatment of animals by humans, the suffering and compassion starts to come into focus. Spirituality is a natural path to overcoming or dealing with suffering and being in harmony with nature, with everything. **And the more harmonious and compassionate you are, ultimately the more enjoyable your life will be.**

The tattoo of stars on my feet were done after I finished school. I was in Byron Bay and I had just deferred going to university. I was feeling challenged at leaving the institution called school. But not yet ready to go into another! I've also been dancing since I was four years old, and I performed and did jazz ballet and tap classes for fifteen years. So the stars on my feet are a kind of homage to that part of my history too. I had the tattoo on my shoulder done when I was eighteen years old. It is taken from the blank rune that is named "ODEN". I had this one done because it stands for **allowing your destiny to unfold** and letting your life unfold in an organic way. **I think it's working so far.**

AGFA APX 100 2 678-20 22R 3 AGFA APX 100

20
RGS

NAME: ANIKA MOA
D.O.B: 21.05.80
AGE: 24 YEARS OLD
NATIONALITY: NEW ZEALAND CITIZEN
LIVES: AUCKLAND, NEW ZEALAND
OCCUPATION: SINGER / SONGWRITER / MUSICIAN

HER STORY:

I first met Anika on the K-Road in Auckland, New Zealand, outside a nightclub where she was due to perform. On this particular night she was singing backup at a gig for friends of hers, in the band "Dimmer". Leading us all the way backstage, Anika told me over her shoulder it was the first time she'd been on stage for a while and she was nervous! She said laughing, "Well at least you'll see me in a dress. I hardly ever get dressed up!" It was clear she had no need to be nervous for she has the most exquisite voice and a natural stage presence. Preferring to be barefoot while performing, Anika is already a star in her native country. Her Maori and English background give her a dual sense of belonging and undoubtedly her sense of purpose. Anika has been given that rare thing, an invitation from one of the leading music companies in the world to become an internationally famous singer / songwriter. It's an invitation she's yet to take up fully. She's so earthy and real - she's the type of girl both men and women love. She's also the kind of girl everyone wants to be friends with, and yet she's not the least bit interested in fame or riches. Anika just loves what she does.

I MIGHT BE A BITCH [LAUGHS] BUT I'M STILL COOL!

My Mum is English, she came from England when she was fourteen. She married my older brother and sister's father who was a Pakeha [white]. So she had two kids to him and then divorced him. Then she married my Dad who was Maori and had two children with him and then divorced him. Then she had a relationship with my younger brother's Dad for about eight years and separated from him. She's had six children from three relationships. And now she's getting married again! She's marrying a gorgeous Maori guy so she's lucky and she's inherited two of his children so…

I only met my father when I was eleven – actually he kind of kidnapped me. [laughs] My Mum and my Dad were together for four years. He's a real Maori, proud but alcohol gets involved and well … and he used to get into trouble with the police.

Out of the blue one day he came and picked me up and said, "You're coming to live with me". I trusted him, I had already met him by this time and he was giving me money and candy and stuff, so I was like, this is sweet! [laughs] A couple of days later I started crying for my Mum. [laughs] I went home but later I agreed to go with him to his family [Puhoro], way up north in the North Island of New Zealand.

Being from Christchurch in the south, which is more conservative and white, that was exciting to me. I'm Maori, **I'm "brown", but up north, I'm "white" to them. [laughs] Because I'm brown in Christchurch, which is where I'm from, I'm not accepted but up north where my family is from, I'm not brown enough!**

The first time I went to the North Island I met all my aunties and uncles and they were laughing about me being the white girl from Christchurch. [laughs] I embrace and accept both my cultures though. I love being English and I love being Maori. I like Maori because it's a very welcoming culture, very open. The bad side is the violence, lots of physical abuse and alcohol. But that can be found in every culture really.

I went to a low to middle class kind of school, heaps of Maori, some Pakeha, and smoking pot was normal in my world. Everyone around me and in my family was smoking pot. I started smoking pot when I was thirteen and I stopped smoking at about sixteen or seventeen. School was the thing I was most passionate about and at school my best subjects were Maori culture and music and I wanted to be able to do them well. I hated school and the only reason I wanted to stay was for those two things. I just didn't need it [pot] any more. It's not a part of my life. It got boring. [laughs]

My Grandad's tribe [Iwi] - right up the top of the North Island is Te Aupouri and it's my main tribe, because it's the paternal line and my sub-tribe [Hapu] is my Nana's tribe is Nga Puhi from the west side. Traditionally the female line is considered to be the sub-tribe. I have respect for my ancestors, even though it's a male dominated culture and there are a few problems with the issue of respect for women. **Women still can't speak at a Marae [sacred gathering place for Maori]. *WHALE RIDER* WAS A PERFECT FILM, IT WAS SO POSITIVE AND A COMPLETELY BEAUTIFUL FILM. It moved us all forward in a beautiful positive way.**

There are a lot of very angry Maori men who have been frustrated for a long time because of the fact that they lost their land. But if the men would heal themselves there would be a better future for all their children. We've all been affected and on occasion beaten, and we were always around too much alcohol and drugs. It was something we all got used to growing up. But you can't use anger as a way of releasing things. So that has to change for the benefit of all of us.

I got my first Moko [tattoo] on my lower wrist when I was eighteen, which is the legal age you are allowed to get a tattoo. My tattoos have all been done in stages. I have my Maori heritage on my arms to remind me. I have koru [the circled curvy lines] for my Mum and Dad, and for when I went to New York. I got one done to remind me of where I'm from - my friends and family in Christchurch. I have my tribal ancestry, my Whakapapa which is my family tree, my country and the land of New Zealand, represented. I have some decorative bits, there to represent my girly feminine side too. I love being girly!

Lately I have been doing different things not so much my own music. I enjoy dressing up to sing with my friend's band! It's quite different to what I do. My music is pretty much me sitting down with a guitar and writing out lyrics and then I put melodies to it. Just singer/songwriter stuff. I write about family mostly. I write about love a little bit but not much because relationships always fuck me over, and I always get bored with them or always get upset so I don't like talking about them! [laughs] I'd rather write something positive. Also women always get classified musically as being "angsty". I would rather write about history and the stories of our past.

I'd rather have my music be in a positive light instead of anything negative.

I learned guitar from my Dad, he taught me when I met him, so music is in my family. He's a musician. My Nana from England was a wonderful singer, she used to be the head of the choir. My Mum also has a beautiful voice and we sing and play together at weddings and gatherings. My Mum loves me and she always just wants me to be happy. She may not understand everything about me but she loves and accepts all my choices. She gets where I'm at, it's cool. **One day I'd like to have a big tribe of my own, ten kids would be great!**

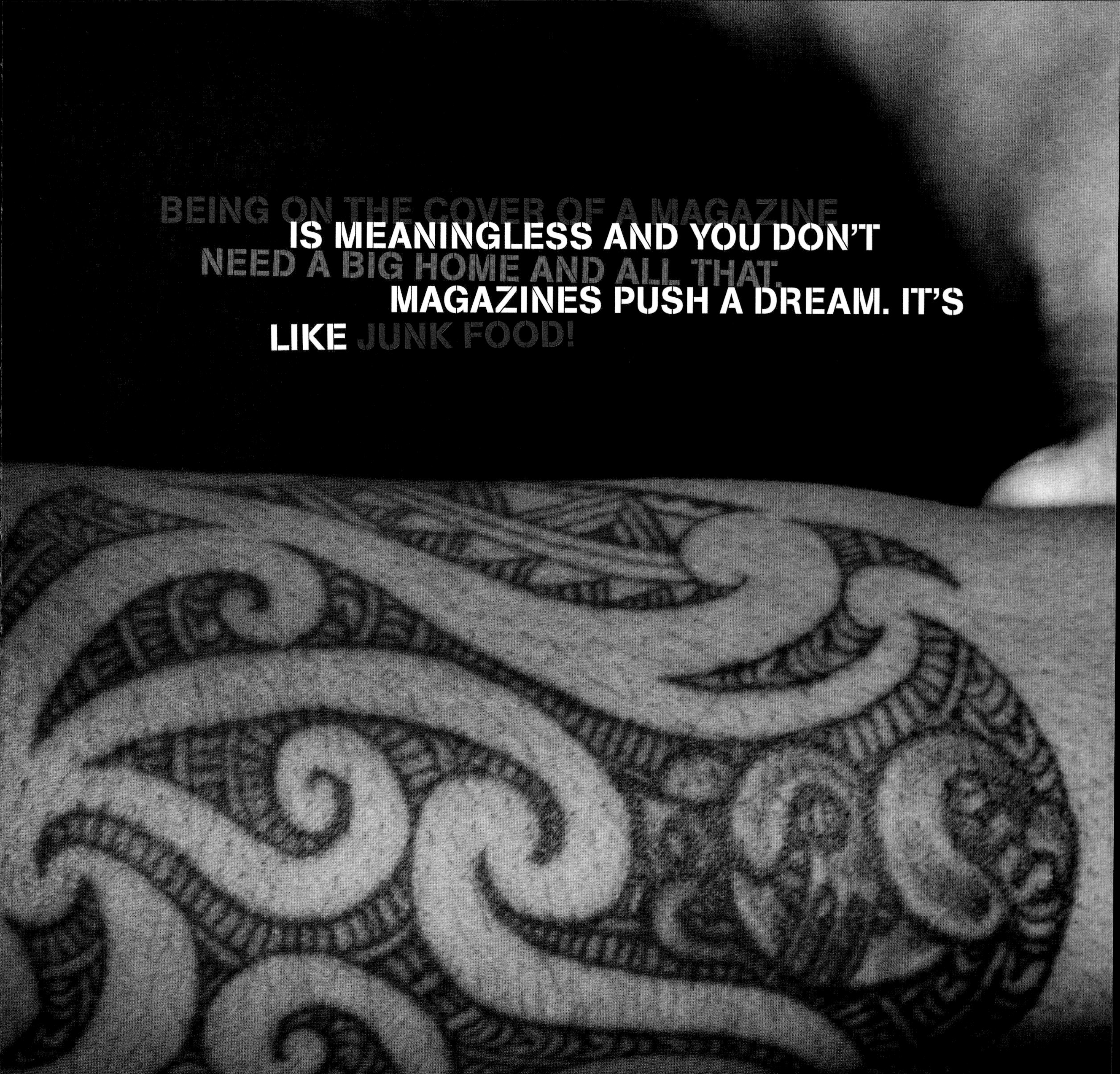

BEING ON THE COVER OF A MAGAZINE IS MEANINGLESS AND YOU DON'T NEED A BIG HOME AND ALL THAT. MAGAZINES PUSH A DREAM. IT'S LIKE JUNK FOOD!

I don’t care about money. I don’t have any. [laughs] Who cares? I’ve got what I need.

Family is the most important draw for me. As far as my roots are concerned, I don't know my North Island family as well as I'd like to, but they respect me for what I'm doing and I respect them. The land is incredible here in New Zealand and that inspires me so much and I feel a part of it.

At the age of eighteen I went in a rock competition down south and a record company in Auckland said they would sign me. I was invited to do an album and I told them that I would wait until I had finished school. I just wanted to finish my studies. Then after school I moved up to Auckland and got signed there. Then I went to New York and I was signed to Atlantic Records. I recorded my album in New York and I moved there to New York City for six months to record it and work with the producer Victor Van Vugt. I called my first album *Thinking Room*. I released the album in America, Australia and here. It didn't do all that well and even if I had toured it for two years it wouldn't have done that well, it wasn't a touring kind of album really.

I went to America for two months and promoted it and did all the magazines and that kind of thing but I didn't like it. I couldn't bear people saying to me all the time, "You're gonna be so famous, you'll be rich, you'll be able to do this and do that!"

I went into it thinking, "okay … if I promote this album for two years maybe I'll be able to buy my Mum a house and maybe I'll end up getting some freak appearance on David Letterman and it will all happen …" [laughs] But actually, at the end of the two months I was over it all. I toured it in 2002 in Australia and New Zealand. I toured with Chris Isaak, I loved being on tour with Chris! It was great going on tour with him because he got really cool crowds. The worst crowd I've ever performed at was in Byron Bay [Australia]. They were shouting "Show us your tits", it was pretty bad!

New York is great - what you see is what you get - and it's real, but that's not all of the country. I was glad to come home! My record label would like to tour me in America. They always say to me "When you're ready to come over, come over". I'm not ready to do that yet. **And I think fame is a bullshit concept. People should stop worshiping fake people and worship real people such as doctors and people like that instead.** Most people are cool here in New Zealand, you've got everything you want right here. You've got beautiful land, you've got friends and family - even if you're poor they'll look after you - and that's cool. So you don't need much. What more do you want?

I was baptized a Catholic when I was seven. I don't really remember it. I don't really understand why either 'cos it's only me and my younger brother who were baptized Catholic! I loved the singing in Church, but once I was old enough to understand what I was singing about, I changed my opinion a bit. Religion is an amazing ideal but it's just "talk story" - you know it's a great story. And it's always subject to interpretation. But I'm Maori, I just believe in being nice to people, try to be happy, to love people. That's my religion, it's simple. You don't judge people. That's just common sense. I don't understand people who hate other people for any reason. It's to each their own, if you ask me.

NAME: SHELLEY LOMAS
D.O.B: 02.05.04
AGE: 19 YEARS OLD
NATIONALITY: NEW ZEALAND CITIZEN
LIVES: AUCKLAND, NEW ZEALAND
OCCUPATION: LAW STUDENT / RESTAURANT HOSTESS

HER STORY:

Shelley Lomas is the type of girl you just know has a lot to say. A second-year science / law student at Auckland University, she is of Indian and New Zealand descent. Sitting in a Moroccan restaurant in the heart of Auckland, she is completely at home in the Middle Eastern setting. Laughing, she says that on a recent trip to Spain, tourists would come up to her and ask for directions. Born in Dubai, Shelley is used to being taken for other nationalities. As naturally gorgeous as she is brainy, Shelley is not the type to rely on her appearance, even when she was offered the chance to cash in on it through modeling. It's not something that would even occur to her. She's not that type of girl!

I grew up as the only child of my parents. My Mum is Indian and my Dad is a Kiwi [New Zealander], and they met in the Middle East and that was where I was born. I was born in Dubai.

My parents lived there for a couple of years but then my father thought the lifestyle in New Zealand was better for bringing up children and so we moved here. My Dad is an accountant from the south and my Mum is now a psychologist. She works with drug and alcohol patients. My Dad used to do a lot of the work for the sheiks in their property developments. Dad used to talk about the crazy parties that went on there. And Mum used to talk about all the drugs that were going on behind the scenes! My Mum's family come from India. I love going there, it's amazing! They live in the south of India, in Bangalore.

My parents split up when I was ten years old. I live with my father and his new partner, who had four sons. One of her sons died, he drowned when he was eighteen. The whole family was distraught about that. My Dad was fantastic with his partner when she lost her son. I was proud of him in the way he interacted with her and looked after her throughout that period. I was glad for her that she had that. He was very caring and supportive. It was good to see.

My Mum is fantastic too. I love her to bits, although I have only recently forged a better relationship with her in recent years. I was very angry with her for ages over the breakup. Age gives you perspective though and you realize that it really isn't anyone's fault. And she's so amazing, such a great mother. We talk a lot about her work. We talk about how people get sucked into certain lifestylse. Alcoholism is a disease. It can be inherited too. A lot of alcoholism is caused from deep-seated insecurities and family background problems, and a lot of it is the bottling up of emotions. My Mum really believes in talking about problems and getting everything out in the open, expressing things and not keeping your problems to yourself. **It's all about clear communication.**

My Mum is my role model because she is so strong. I tend to look at other people and take the things I admire in them. Right now life is about experiencing new things and learning new lessons. I have always enjoyed my life. It is something to be embraced.

We have been having lots of discussions about not comparing yourself to other people. We talk about living your own life and doing what you have to do and trying to find yourself and just building nice relationships along the way. The main thing that Mum has told me about addictions and problems of that nature is that **you can only solve problems by yourself**. A quick fix of any substance will not help you to solve any of the internal problems. It's hard but you have to deal with those internal issues. Here in Auckland there is a drug called 'P', which has a bit of a reputation for inducing aggression in users. Mum is getting very worried about the use of ecstasy. She is particularly worried about the backyard manufacturing of it. People don't know what they are taking, and it could have anything in it!

I BELIEVE IN REINCARNATION AND
KARMA. WHAT YOU GIVE IS EXACTLY
WHAT YOU GET. EVEN IN THIS LIFE.
I HAVE CHOSEN THAT BELIEF.

There is a lot of information out there about drugs but you have to be careful these days. There are ramifications, and everyone wants to experiment and of course they think that they are invincible. But everyone should think of the ramifications more. **You always think you have the rest of your life, but you may not.**

I have looked at a lot of religions and I think you take the bits from each one that you feel work for you. I believe in the Universe. You have to be conscious of other people and aware of them in all respects. Try and do your best for other people and not be mean. It's cool to be kind! It takes a conscious effort but I think it's essential. You create your own reality. Everyone has their reality. And you must respect the reality of the next person!

I am in my second year of university studying Science Law at Auckland University. I was thinking about specializing in patent law, but I'm not quite decided. It's a five-year course so I still have time to think about it. My law degree is a means to an end. It's quite philosophical in content. I enjoy discussing a lot of the moral issues. I love science. That is my passion. I would hate to be stuck in a lab though! I love dealing with people. I work in a bar as a waitress three times a week, and I work as a hostess out the front and try and entice them in. I love it! But it's unbelievable what you see in a bar. The mating game in action is so funny to watch! It's completely different from university and that's refreshing.

Because I am from the Middle East, I think the whole situation over there with the war is really sad. The plight of women is so bad. The rape statistics, the abuse, wages are really appalling. I feel for women in that region. They don't have their freedom and the rest of the world has progressed so much.

I don't know about love. It's important and it hits you when you don't expect it! I am in a relationship at the moment. My boyfriend is an English teacher, he helps immigrants when they come into the country to learn English, which is cool.

I WAS ASKED TO BE A MODEL WHEN I WAS YOUNG. IT NEVER APPEALED TO ME. When I was young I was really insecure about how I looked and I didn't want to expose myself. It epitomizes what I don't think is important about life. It's does nothing for most people's self-esteem. I think it's sad when young girls aspire to being a model. I always want to ask them, **"Why do you want to be beautiful?** Do you think it will make you a better person? Does that mean you'll enjoy yourself? Do you think it will make you happy?" Beauty is so fleeting. And modeling is basically really fake. It's not real! So many women are beautiful and that should be embraced, but what society deems beautiful is just so narrow, it doesn't cater for any sort of differences.

My parents have always told me I am smart and told me to try all sorts of things to do with art and learning. My Mum won a beauty contest in Dubai in the seventies and she was on the cover of magazines and stuff, but she felt it was a degrading experience. She didn't want that for me so she was always really wary of the whole modeling thing for me. She would hate for me to get hurt in anyway. I said no. I had a lot of friends who did do the modeling thing and even though we have the similar background we have kind of drifted apart.

All my friends today think in the same way I do about these things! BUT MAYBE IF YOU GIVE OUT A CERTAIN AURA THAT'S THE KIND OF PEOPLE YOU ATTRACT.

It appears a lot of people think the mantra for today is "Do what society thinks is right, make some money and have some kids! Be beautiful the whole time, while you're doing the laundry and making your husband's dinner and having your career!" [laughs] That's the popular version of what you're meant to do.

Riding horses in my childhood was a big thing. I was really happy as a child. I never wanted to grow up, but the standout moments have often been negative. The moments that have stood out for me have always been on a long horse ride with friends or even by myself. Being out there and seeing beautiful sunsets. Those times are really important memories. They are precious to me. Horse riding took the focus off any insecurity about your looks - it was about grooming your horse and having friends and being in a group activity. I always loved school though. **I WAS A BIT OF A NERD! I WAS NEVER UNCOOL OR OUT OF FAVOR WITH ANYONE.** My friends and I just did our own thing. We were almost isolated in a way.

Another great memory is going to Spain and Portugal with my Mum a couple of years ago. We went to Madrid first. My Mum's health isn't so great at the moment. She suffers from arthritis and it's hard for her to get around easily. So going to Spain for us was such a lovely experience. It didn't matter that I didn't speak any Spanish. In fact most people thought I was Spanish. Everyone was so nice, hot weather, great wine and food. I'm trying to learn a bit of Spanish, I did a basic course so now I need to go over and immerse myself. I'd like to go traveling around South America next!

My future seems uncertain. I don't know where I'm going or what I'm doing really. [laughs] I think I have changed since I made the decision to do this course. As much as I enjoy the studying, I can't see what I'm going to use it for in my future.

I believe in giving back. It's very important. You gain so much from doing so and being aware of what's going on in the world. Helping other people in their lives, and trying to improve their position. That's the whole karma thing. **Make people happy and you'll get it back for yourself.**

Guys are always looking for what they want. I've never found any good relationships in bars when guys are just looking for a certain type.

NAME: SAM SYMONDS
D.O.B: 23.06.72
AGE: 32 YEARS OLD
NATIONALITY: ENGLISH
LIVES: CAMBRIDGE, UK
OCCUPATION: CHILDREN'S ENTERTAINER/ ARTIST

I am a fairy princess [laughs]

HER STORY:

I first met Sam near the end of her year-long trip. Having traveled through South America, Australia and New Zealand and braved arduous (and dubious!) transport means across all countries (and survived), Sam was what you might call the typical English backpacker. With her dreadlocked hair and easy-going nature - not to mention her willingness to "rough it" hostel-style - it would be easy to make assumptions. In reality, Sam is anything but typical and what makes her so unusual is not what can be assessed on first impressions. Sam loves fairies - she calls herself a fan of "nature spirits" - and is a gifted artist who renders imaginative scenes which take the viewer back to a forgotten childhood. Where other people take happy snaps of their trips, Sam had painted hers. Her journal was a thing of wonder containing the most exquisite water colors and illustrations of places and people whom she had met on her personal magic carpet ride.

Upon her return to her home in the United Kingdom, Sam completed the transformation, begun in the previous years of traveling, in becoming a Professional Fairy for children's parties. In this role, she is perfect and her elfin features and toothy smile combine in just the way you'd imagine a fairy - if you happened upon one in real life!

Sam lives and works in the realm of imagination, which fuels her work and makes others happy - **surely the purest form of magic** - and a much-needed contribution to the world.

I live one hour north of London, near Cambridge, the town of Cambridge University. It's quite rural where I'm from, the area is known for the horseracing scene, but my family upbringing was more of "small town" than rural as such. I didn't go to London until I was nineteen and I enrolled at Kingston University in Surrey to study graphic design. So my first experience of a big city and of living out of home was while I was studying – I lived on campus for about a year.

My outstanding memory of my childhood was that it was stable and very creative. My parents are both really creative people … my Dad used to be a carpenter and a builder and wood-turning is his hobby. He's always mucking around with bits and pieces of wood. It's not work for him, he does it because he loves doing it. My Mum is really good at knitting and sewing - she makes clothes and is a talented dressmaker and costume designer. They also always encouraged me — and my younger sister and brother too — to be interested in and take inspiration from nature.

I think that with those influences from an early age, I was bound to turn out creative in some way! I always wanted to be an artist of some sort, and my course was split into two strands – graphic design or illustration. I chose graphic design, however I should have chosen illustration in retrospect … Anyone who sees my work always asks if I'm an illustrator of children's books. That is my ultimate dream.

I went to see some publishers in London recently. It came to pass in the most bizarre way though! I was staying with a friend and I accidentally got stuck in a hallway – I was locked out of the apartment and locked inside the building – and so I had about three hours to kill. I had my mobile phone with me so I decided to make good use of the time and make some calls to publishers. I decided to make some good come out of a bad situation!

I made the appointment and I went along very casually. I had no preconceptions or expectations. The meeting was amazing - eventually quite a group had gathered around my portfolio and they were calling in their colleagues to have a look. I was just excited that they were excited! But part of me was still thinking "Shouldn't this be a bit harder?"

But maybe I was thinking that because my life at times has felt like it was hard. Especially since I came back from my trip. I came home and was like, "I'm thirty-two, I'm back living with my parents and I'm not getting anywhere – I'm on the scrap heap!" Before I moved in I very selfishly and big-headedly thought it would be nice for my parents, that maybe they could learn something from me! You know, as parents do learn from their children. But we have had disagreements – which is only natural among adults really – and so it hasn't always gone as I thought. I think it's hard for my parents generation – they don't always understand that you can be single, wear dreadlocks and be happy with not necessarily having a stable home all the time.

I'm cancerian and I like my home. I actually love a bit of stability and having everything in its place. I can't wait to have a place of my own, but it may not happen for a while as I have also been trying to get my new business off the ground. The business I'm building is as a Professional Fairy for children's parties. It has been a hard slog really. But my Mum has helped me to design and make my costume, so that's been a lovely project for us both to work on.

Fairies are not necessarily
little winged beings at the bottom
of the garden – this is just the
popular image that appeals
both adults and
I believe they are nature spiri
maybe a kind of energetic force
behind everything in the natural
world.

People always ask me if I was always interested in fairies, and they are surprised when I tell them "No, not at all!" [laughs]

My interest in fairies is a recent thing, and it came as a result of my trip to Australia and New Zealand, specifically a place called Bellingen – in the north of New South Wales, in Australia. I felt drawn to the small town of Bellingen on an earlier trip. I just knew it was a magical place. I was staying with a family and for some reason during that period I began to draw and paint fairies. I was drawn to it – literally! So that was the beginning of the journey, which developed further in New Zealand, which is so beautiful – the landscape there is so lush – it's another magical place. Also with the *Lord of the Rings* being filmed there and the whole "Elf" thing going on, it was that kind of energy all around me… You can't get away from it there!

Since I've been home I have now come across a whole fairy network. It can get pretty interesting! Some people say they have seen them, but I've never seen a fairy – unless you can call seeing them in my mind in order to paint them, seeing them. I don't believe they sit at the bottom of the garden as some people do. Being a Professional Fairy for children is my way of celebrating the nature spirits. They love the idea of fairies and elves – it is something that all children really relate to.

I realized that I needed to get out and spend more time with like-minded people. I was spending a lot of time cooped up and I felt isolated. I was probably a bit depressed but I just needed to re-connect and see friends really. I needed to make new friends too, who were more on my wavelength.

I guess I had drifted apart a bit from my university friends… they all have nice flats or houses, partners and corporate careers. I didn't feel like that was "me" but I didn't know who I was! I suppose mostly I thought I no longer fit into their lives. I kept feeling that if I should be earning lots of money and that I should have what they all have, but making the steps towards my dream shows me that I'm fine the way I am. Now they tell me "You've got all this talent and you're starting your own business, **so it's a fantastic opportunity, it's really exciting". It was an eye opener to find that they were a bit envious of me!**

I was so surprised. I have now come to appreciate that everyone changes and sometimes you evolve in the same direction but often you go in a new and different direction. But you can always re-connect.

I never imagined myself as a children's entertainer, but it feels like I'm on a roll now! I'm starting to get my business through word-of-mouth and I now have several parties in pre-production. The children love it and it really inspires them, which feels rewarding.

Traveling is one of the best things you can do if you want to jump start a new direction in life.

Wings are symbolic – when I put on a pair of fairy wings, I immediately feel different; more joyful and confident, and they certainly bring a smile to people's faces.

It seems to me that working with children keeps you young, while having children makes you grow up.

Faerie-Sam

Nowadays when children ask if I'm a real fairy, I tell them, "No I'm not, but I work for the fairies." My job is to spread their message that we must look after our environment.

I went on my last trip – which at eighteen months was the longest I've done – feeling fed up with life in London and not knowing what I wanted yet knowing I needed to get out. The most outstanding thing that has come from my trip is what I'm doing creatively and professionally. The alternative was living my old life and being dissatisfied.

I believe in having general aims in life, but I also believe you shouldn't worry too much about the path that you take to get there. It's still worth it no matter how long it takes. I don't believe in the five-year plan because if you don't do it, you'll disappoint yourself. **Another thing I have learned is that you are not your friends so don't compare yourself to them or to what they have. They are on their own journey!**

There will always be those chance meetings in life, I call them angels – those people you meet who show you the way. I've been so lucky, I have had a few of those. They are the ones who speak to you and you just know it's a message being channeled! Even if you only meet them for five minutes, you somehow know they were sent.

I had that exact experience in November 2003. I had a stall at an art fair with the cards, illustrations, prints and mirrors I had made. I am always looking for ways to put my energies onto things so they will sell! I was in my fairy outfit and this woman came by and started to tell me about how she and her husband had started their business with her husband's art. I told her about a part-time job I have at this place in a forest and how I really believe it's essential to get people closer to nature again. I could tell from the way she was talking to me that she really got who I was and what I was all about. Then she said the most amazing thing to me. "The fairies are the only thing holding this world together." I got pretty emotional, I started crying. It was such a release for me to have someone connect with me on that level. It was a message for me personally and it was only brief, but she was an angel.

Only you can follow your path in life. Whatever you do is right for you – it might not be right for someone else.

NAME: TRACY DAWN ESPINOSA
D.O.B: 08.08.72
AGE: 32 YEARS OLD
NATIONALITY: U.S. CITIZEN
LIVES: OKLAHOMA CITY, UNITED STATES
OCCUPATION: PERSONAL ASSISTANT

HER STORY:

Tracy Dawn is one of those people whom you listen to when she speaks. A gentle soul, Tracy has had such an extreme childhood that her well-adjusted manner is all the more noteworthy. But Tracy Dawn is surprising at every turn. More than just a survivor, she has done the textbook "life turnaround" and in such conditions that you can only marvel at the strength of the human spirit.

I have never met Tracy Dawn, but we already feel that we know each other, thanks to a generous use of the telephone and the written word. She is a worthy inclusion in this book because of her approach to life. Her wisdom and compassion are the product of all that she has experienced, and a lesson to each of us about the power of forgiveness. Tracy Dawn has transcended.

I was born and have lived in Oklahoma city, Oklahoma, all my life. I have one brother and one sister. I am the eldest child in our family. My father is Mexican, although he was born in the United States. I don't know my mother's heritage. She was fair skinned with red hair and green eyes. She was abandoned by her mother, and her father committed suicide when she was twelve years old. My mother did not really know her own heritage. Whenever I asked her what nationality she thought she was she claimed to have a little Cherokee [Native American Indian], black Dutch and Irish.

My family was extremely poor and my childhood was filled with disturbing incidences of abandonment, neglect, frequent homelessness, poverty and traumatic and persistent drama. At some points in my childhood, the only thing that I had as support was the idea I held that there was a special plan for my life. At times, this idea was the only "personal property" I possessed.

My father was an alcoholic. He and my mother were never married and my Mom was sixteen when I was born. My parents lived together off and on throughout my life. My mother was herself addicted to drugs and this was the case throughout my life. Every so often my mother would pack us up and take us somewhere else to live.

I saw my first dead body when I was five or six years old. It was an overdose victim in a run down hotel apartment where we were staying. We used to follow the cleaning lady around to entertain ourselves and the victim was in one of the rooms we went into. I witnessed overdoses of my mother so many times when we were younger. We'd have to call an ambulance and they would come and get us from whatever hotel she had us staying at.

My siblings and I were put into foster homes for a while and then later were returned to the custody of our parents. The home we lived in for the longest period of time was less than four hundred square feet with only one room. WHEN WE MOVED IN IT HAD ABSOLUTELY NO PLUMBING, WINDOWS, HEATING OR AIR CONDITIONING. FOR AT LEAST THE FIRST YEAR WE CARRIED WATER FROM THE NEIGHBOR'S HOUSE FOR DRINKING and we took baths once a week at the homes of friends or relatives. Even in these conditions I managed to win two essay contests at the age of eight and nine. I asked my school for permission to start a cheerleading squad and they approved it. Through the chaos of my childhood these small accomplishments were significant. They were further proof to me of my purpose and they prodded me to press on.

I think my Mom did every drug at one stage or another. I was about eighteen when I learned that she was taking major street drugs. In later life, my mother started using heroin. She was thirty-five at the time she became a heroin addict. And after that we would often find her homeless on the street.

Because of my mother's lifestyle, we met so many people. They were all involved in the drug scene. They used to hang out in a group. Some of them were amazingly creative and interesting. They could have made contributions, but ultimately addicts are more self-destructive than creative. They could all have chosen another path, but the primary contributing factor to addiction is a low self-esteem coupled with a bad environment.

Nobody wants to die, and no one really wants to be an addict and to be defeated in that way.

At eighteen, when I was staying at my Dad's place, I decided to move out. I was getting tired and I knew I would never graduate unless I did something for myself. My Mom was pretty bad at this point. I kept up with my studies all through the difficult times.

During my high school years I made very good grades. I was an officer in our Junior Navy ROTC [Reserve Officers Training Corps]. I was a cheerleader despite the fact that we were so poor that I only had two pairs of socks. **I so much wanted to participate in these school activities that I asked people to sponsor me.** This was how I bought my uniforms. To those who helped me, I will be forever grateful.

After high school I got married. We were too young however and we were divorced five years later. In my young adult life, some of the scars of my past began to resurface and I made some very expensive mistakes. Some were unintended and some were desperately pre-calculated. But I still had successes that kept me going, and kept me believing there was a higher purpose for my life.

I was an honor student at Oklahoma State University and I volunteered for many organizations. The thing that makes me most proud was becoming one of the first missionary interns with an organization called "Way of the Cross". We built houses for people who lived in a dump in Matamoras in Mexico.

When I was twenty-seven years old, I went on staff as the Director of Local Services with a local organization in Bridgecreek, Oklahoma called Bartimeus Ministries Inc. **I HELPED THEM BECOME A NATIONALLY RECOGNIZED NON-PROFIT ORGANIZATION.**

While I was there, I started a small community food pantry. When, in 1999 our community was hit by a F-5 [force five] tornado, our headquarters was positioned perfectly to help organize a huge recovery effort.

I then helped to raise over US$230,000 for the victims, so they could rebuild their homes.

Oklahoma has been an interesting place to live, although it has had problems in recent years. When the Oklahoma bombing happened in 1997, I was in Stillwater about forty-five minutes away. We couldn't make phone calls - all the lines were down - and my family all thought my sister was around the area where the bomb went off. The authorities had blocked off the city and so that was really scary. But it turned out my sister had slept through a doctor's appointment and so thankfully she wasn't in the impact zone. Sadly about one hundred and seventy other people were killed. The biggest shift in consciousness after that was that we had terrorist activity on U.S. soil. **We had not fully appreciated how very protected America is from actions that many countries in the world experience on a daily basis.**

I am:
a leo
loyal
diverse
loving
out going
strong minded
passionate
determined
tenacious
trustworthy
full of life

NO MATTER WHAT YOUR CIRCUMSTANCES, YOU STILL CHOOSE YOUR LIFE.

The good thing was that it brought people together and underlined the strong sense of community that truly exists here but the downside is that people lock their doors now.

Everyone says that the reason I have not yet had children is that I was a parent since I was a kid and I raised my Mom and Dad. **But the main thing is to look back and understand why things happen.** My parents both had harrowing histories of their own. For some reason when I was really young I knew that survival would depend on me parenting my parents.

I still see my Dad and my sister. But I don't see my brother as often as I would like to. Mom died in March 2003. She was taking methadone and heroin and she overdosed. My father is having a hard time with the loss of my mother. He has been sober for ten years now. He has become a nomadic truck driver. He always kept a steady job - at least he went to work. My parents were never very spiritual but now he calls me and says, "Your mother's here …"

We need to educate parents that they can deliver crushing self-esteem blows to children. They often do so without realizing. We need to help people find out individually what is blocking self-esteem and to interact with others on a healthy level. My Mom was introduced to drugs at the age of fifteen. She could barely read or write and she didn't know anything else. She thought she had no other options. We need to educate people on what their options are and to help them - support them - to find what works for them. In five years I want to become a life coach. I would like to give non-judgemental advice. I would love to be someone they can bounce ideas off - and to help them to find themselves.

I am happy with myself. And whether it was my own strength or someone else's, I am amazed at how much I have done. There has been a force protecting me, of that much I am certain.

The adversity I have had in my life has made me who I am.

THANKYOUS

Thank you to everyone who participated in and contributed to **REALGIRLS'STORIES**.

To my support crew: Many thanks for always being there and for also supplying much-needed caffeine, trashies, shoulders, tech support, dinners and phone calls, text messages or emails which made me laugh. Mum and Dad, Carole Muller, Justine O'Donnell, Skye Gunning, Susi Stitt, Cath Derksema, Nadine Bush, Chris Cudlip, Bianca & Dave Wesson, Jessica Adams, Bec Hanlon, Nick Carroll, Mel Woolfe, Fi Coogan, Jaime Marina, Jodie Cooper & Lili Munoz, Lisa Reynolds, Sally Prisk, Simon & Sue Blundell, Kelly McCoy, and Tracy Simpson.

To Justine O'Donnell of jmedia design: To the other half of my brain (the really good bit). Many thanks Jusi, for your energy and brilliance, your friendship and your dedication.

To Brent Spencer-Young of The Sydney Darkroom: For the beautiful black & white prints, for the endless cups of tea and for your friendship. You are an artist.

Many thanks for all the help backstage: To the team at Allen & Unwin, Jennifer Darling, Campbell Murray Creating, Allens Arthur Robinson (Jackie O'Brien & Miriam Stiel), John Martin, Marnie Neck, Will Cate, Jamie Durie, Greg Daniel, Harry Miller.

To my editors and friends in the surfing world, thanks for your patience while I dropped off the radar. Can't wait to see you all again!

Special thanks to all the 'real girls' who gave generously with their enthusiasm, their time and - on occasion - their photo archives.

To my beautiful Drew, your love makes it all worthwhile. Thanks for looking after me, for taking me surfing, for making me laugh even at five a.m. … and for always picking me up from the airport.

PHOTOGRAPHY CREDITS

RGS photography by Anthea Paul. Copyright © Anthea Paul.

ADDITIONAL PHOTOGRAPHY CREDITS

Pages 10-11	Sean Davey
Page 14	Kin Kimoto
Page 32	photographs courtesy of Radha Melis
Pages 36-41	photographs courtesy of the Uhlmann family
Pages 42-49	Photographs by Andre B. Murray
Pages 72-77	Briar Shaw
Pages 84-85	strip of images center page: Dave Stewart
Page 120	bottom left-hand image: Loz Smith
Page 121	bottom right-hand image: Steve Doick
Pages 144-153	Ashley de Prazer
Pages 170-175	Briar Shaw
Pages 178-179	photographs courtesy of Sam Symonds
Pages 184-189	photographs courtesy of Tracy Dawn Espinosa

Many thanks to everyone who contributed photos and illustrations to this project. Copyright on additional artwork supplied vests with the artist.

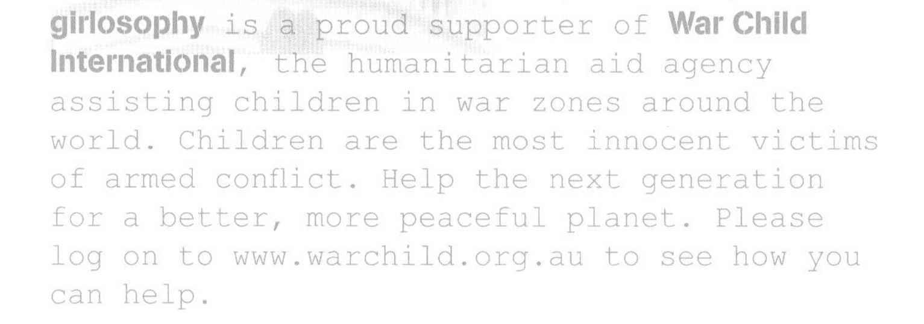

girlosophy is a proud supporter of **War Child International**, the humanitarian aid agency assisting children in war zones around the world. Children are the most innocent victims of armed conflict. Help the next generation for a better, more peaceful planet. Please log on to www.warchild.org.au to see how you can help.

girlosophy is also a proud supporter of the **Tibetan Friendship Group** [TFG], a humanitarian orgnization assisting and rehabilitating Tibetan refugees in India. His Holiness, Dalai Lama is the patron of TFG. Please support this worthy cause. Help TFG restore and preserve the ancient and gentle culture of Tibet. Visit www.tibetan.org.au to send a donation or to see how you can help.

04
RGS
SWITZERLAND
ANJA wants to study here*
AUSTRALIA
18
RGS
ROMY LIVES HERE x
NEW ZEALAND
09
RGS
Susi's red cross shop is here
NORTH ISLAND
NEW ZEALAND
Anikas family come from here*
20
RGS
PERTH
13
RGS
UNITED STATES OF AMERICA
DALIA went to UNIVERSITY here*